**Student Workbook**

# Today's Math

**Daily Practice**

**Mixed Review**

**Test Prep**

**Editorial Offices:** Glenview, Illinois • Parsippany, New Jersey • New York, New York
**Sales Offices:** Needham, Massachusetts • Duluth, Georgia • Glenview, Illinois
Coppell, Texas • Ontario, California • Mesa, Arizona

Created by Pearson Scott Foresman to supplement **Investigations in Number, Data, and Space**®
These materials do not necessarily reflect the opinions or perspective of TERC or the authors of the
*Investigations* curriculum.

ISBN: 0-328-12654-3

5 6 7 8 9 10 V031 13 12 11 10 09 08 07 06 05

# Contents

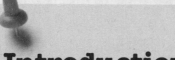

# Introduction

## Why This Book?

**School policies vary widely on issues of homework.** Some teachers are free to assign homework as they see fit, while others are required to assign work every night, every other night, or according to some other schedule depending on the age of their students.

**In order to accommodate the wide range of school and district policies,** enough homework is embedded in the *Investigations* curriculum that a teacher can assign homework about every other night. Furthermore, Practice Pages, Extensions, Classroom Routines (in grades K–2), Ten-Minute Math activities (in grades 3–5), and *Investigations* Games can be used to provide or create additional homework assignments.

**Recently, teachers have expressed a need for an additional resource: grade-specific books that will meet three needs:**

- Relate to the math content of each day's session

- Provide daily practice in number sense and operations

- Help prepare students for standardized testing

This book meets these needs.

- It provides engaging and meaningful practice that will further develop children's understanding of the basic concepts and skills that are currently being taught.

- It gives parents and other caregivers a better sense of what children are doing in math class and over the course of the school year. Most parents understand that "the basics" now encompass all areas of mathematics, not only arithmetic. And many parents are willing, and indeed eager, to help however they can. Therefore, on all student pages there are **Family Connection** notes that give parents the information they need.

- The **Mixed Review and Test Prep** sections help develop computational fluency while preparing students for the language and format of standardized tests. (These sections review concepts and skills that were taught in the previous grade.)

# Family Connection

## Dear Family,

Pearson Scott Foresman is pleased to introduce a new component in your child's mathematics program: Today's Math workbooks.

Sometimes your child will complete a page in class and bring it home to show you. Other times, your child might be assigned a page to complete at home (perhaps with your assistance, as time allows).

## Features of Today's Math

1 The **main activity** relates to the math content of that day's math lesson (or, in some cases, to previous lessons within the current unit).

2 **Mixed Review and Test Prep** exercises prepare your child for standardized testing. Each test-prep item **(a)** helps your child review and maintain basic number skills and concepts learned previously; and **(b)** helps prepare him or her to deal with, and indeed feel comfortable with, the language and format of standardized tests.

3 The **Family Connection** notes will give you **(a)** a "snapshot" of what your child is doing in math class; **(b)** the background you need in order to help your child; **(c)** opportunities to engage in "math conversations" with your child; and **(d)** suggestions for activities you might do together with your child.

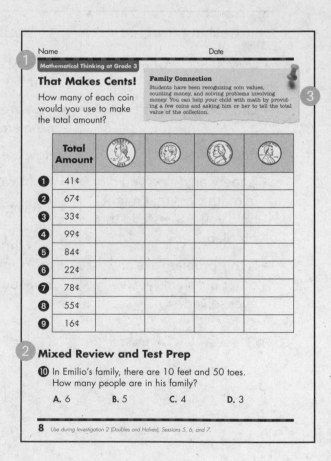

## When Working with Your Child

**Try using some of the sample questions from the chart below.** They can help you start an ongoing math conversation with your child, and they will encourage your child to explain his or her mathematical thinking. It is vitally important that children learn to verbalize their thinking, voice their questions and concerns, and learn to think of themselves as effective and thoughtful problem solvers. Knowing that their parents and teachers value their thinking is very important to children.

**We hope that you will enjoy working on Today's Math with your child. As always, your participation and support are greatly valued and very much appreciated.**

## Having Math Conversations with Your Child

### SAMPLE QUESTIONS

| Getting Started | While Working | Wrapping Up |
|---|---|---|
| • Do you know what to do on this page? | • Do you see any patterns here? | • Why did you decide to solve the problem this way? |
| • Can you explain it to me? | • How are these two problems alike? | • Is there another way to solve this kind of problem? |
| • Is there something you need to find out? | • How are they different? | • How do you know that your answer makes sense? |
| • Is there anything you did in math class that might help you understand this problem? | • What would happen if …? | • What kinds of math problems are easy for you? |
| • Is this problem like any other problems you've ever solved? | • Is this the kind of problem you can do in your head, or is this the kind of problem you need to work out on paper? | • What kinds of problems are hard for you? |

**Mathematical Thinking at Grade 3**

# Show Me 100!

**1** Color 100 cubes.

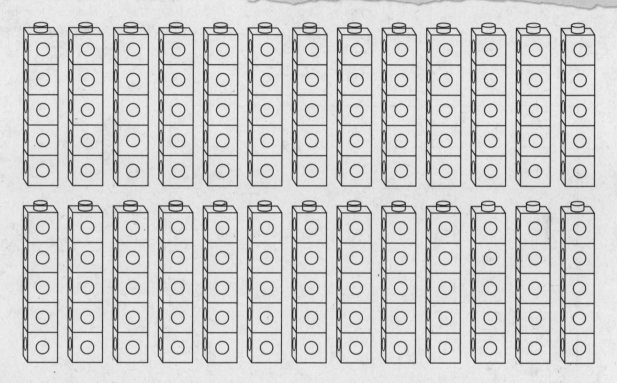

**2** How do you know that you counted exactly 100 cubes?

_____

_____

_____

## Mixed Review and Test Prep

**3** Which does **not** show a way to make 5?

**A.** $2 + 2$     **B.** $3 + 2$     **C.** $6 - 1$     **D.** $10 - 5$

**Mathematical Thinking at Grade 3**

# Missing Numbers

**1** Write these numbers on the 100 chart.

| 34 | 100 | 17 | 22 | 76 |
|----|-----|----|----|----|
| 39 | 44  | 1  | 59 | 45 |
| 16 | 54  | 62 | 88 | 91 |

**Family Connection**

Students have been working with hundred charts. They have used the patterns of numbers in the rows and columns to help them find missing numbers on the charts. **Questions you might ask your child:** "What number is just below 10 on the hundred chart?" (20) "What number is in the box just to the right of 55?" (56)

|    | 2  | 3  | 4  | 5  | 6  | 7  | 8  | 9  |    |
|----|----|----|----|----|----|----|----|----|----|
| 11 |    |    |    |    |    |    |    |    | 20 |
| 21 |    |    |    |    |    |    |    |    | 30 |
| 31 |    |    |    |    |    |    |    |    | 40 |
| 41 |    |    |    |    |    |    |    |    | 50 |
| 51 |    |    |    |    |    |    |    |    | 60 |
| 61 |    |    |    |    |    |    |    |    | 70 |
| 71 |    |    |    |    |    |    |    |    | 80 |
| 81 |    |    |    |    |    |    |    |    | 90 |
|    | 92 | 93 | 94 | 95 | 96 | 97 | 98 | 99 |    |

# Mixed Review and Test Prep

**2** How many more days is it until day 100?

**A.** 20 days    **C.** 10 days

**B.** 15 days    **D.** 5 days

Today's Day
**90**

**Mathematical Thinking at Grade 3**

# 10 More, 10 Less

Finish each row.

**Family Connection**

In this activity, students complete tables to show numbers that are 10 more and 10 less than a given number. You can help your child with math by naming a number between 10 and 90 and asking him or her to tell the numbers that are 10 more and 10 less.

**①**

| | | | | | |
|---|---|---|---|---|---|
| **10 Less Than the Number** | 34 | | | | 1 |
| **The Number** | 44 | 67 | 24 | | |
| **10 More Than the Number** | | | 34 | 26 | 21 |

**②**

| | | | | | |
|---|---|---|---|---|---|
| **10 More Than the Number** | 58 | | | 28 | |
| **10 Less Than the Number** | | 60 | 11 | | 70 |
| **The Number** | | | | 18 | |

**③**

| | | | | | |
|---|---|---|---|---|---|
| **The Number** | 14 | 40 | | | 82 |
| **10 More Than the Number** | 24 | | | 100 | |
| **10 Less Than the Number** | | | 25 | | |

# Mixed Review and Test Prep

**④** Ed, Ron, Jim, Ann, Sue, Judy, Kurt, Linda, Jen, Huong, Ale, and Gloria are wearing blue. Which group of tallies shows the number of people wearing blue?

**A.** 卌 ||     **B.** 卌 卌 |     **C.** 卌 卌 ||     **D.** 卌 卌 |||

**Mathematical Thinking at Grade 3**

# Seeing Doubles

Write the double that matches the design.

**Family Connection**
Students have been working with pattern blocks (flat geometric shapes) to build designs that show doubles, such as 4 + 4. You might want to ask your child to tell you all the doubles he or she knows.

**1**

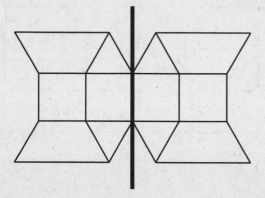

_____ + _____ = _____

**2**

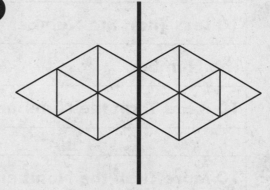

_____ + _____ = _____

**3**

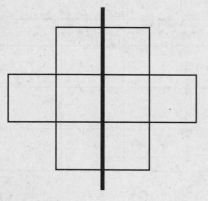

_____ + _____ = _____

**4**

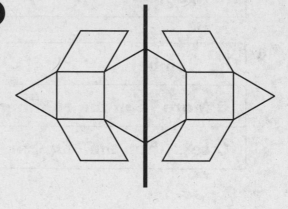

_____ + _____ = _____

# Mixed Review and Test Prep

**5**  ⬜2⬜ , ⬜5⬜ , and ⬜?⬜ make 10.

**A.** ⬜5⬜          **B.** ⬜4⬜          **C.** ⬜3⬜          **D.** ⬜2⬜

# Gone Fishing

**1** Color the doubles yellow.
Color the combinations
of 10 green.

**Family Connection**
Students have been learning
strategies for addition. Two of
the strategies they have been
learning are adding doubles,
such as 3 + 3, and adding combinations of 10, such as 6 + 4.
One way you can help your
child with math is to practice
addition with him or her when-
ever you get the chance.

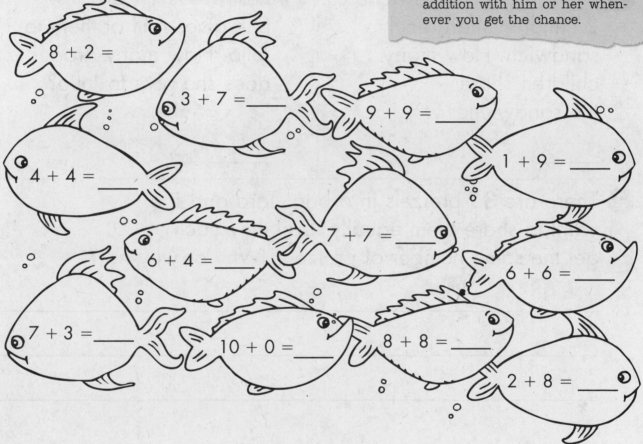

$8 + 2 =$ _____

$3 + 7 =$ _____

$9 + 9 =$ _____

$4 + 4 =$ _____

$1 + 9 =$ _____

$6 + 4 =$ _____

$7 + 7 =$ _____

$6 + 6 =$ _____

$7 + 3 =$ _____

$10 + 0 =$ _____

$8 + 8 =$ _____

$2 + 8 =$ _____

# Mixed Review and Test Prep

**2** Which shape below does **not**
belong in the group?

A.

B.

C.

D.

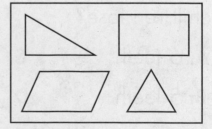

# Double or Divide?

Double or divide to solve each problem.

**Family Connection**

Students are continuing to learn strategies for solving problems. The problems on this page involve doubling a number or dividing a number in half. You might want to ask your child to explain how he or she solved each problem.

**1** There are 11 sandwiches. 2 children share each sandwich. How many children share the sandwiches?

_____

**2** Maria has 14 grapes. She gives half of them to Julio. How many grapes does she give to Julio?

_____

**3** There are 35 pretzels in a bag. Tara and Joe want to share them equally. Can they each get the same number of pretzels? Why or why not?

_____

_____

_____

## Mixed Review and Test Prep

**4** How many teeth did the most children lose?

    **A.** 6 teeth      **C.** 4 teeth

    **B.** 5 teeth      **D.** 3 teeth

**Lost Teeth**

1
2
3
4
5
6

Name _____    Date _____

# My Clues

Write a number combination that gives you a clue to help you solve the problems.

**Family Connection**

Students have been learning to use addition combinations they know to help solve combinations they don't know. For example, $5 + 5 = 10$ can be used to help solve $5 + 6$. The answer is just 1 more than 10.

**1**

$10 + 4 =$

$4 + 10 =$

Clue: _____

Answer: _____

**2**

$6 + 3 =$

$3 + 6 =$

Clue: _____

Answer: _____

**3**

$7 + 6 =$

$6 + 7 =$

Clue: _____

Answer: _____

**4**

$5 + 8 =$

$8 + 5 =$

Clue: _____

Answer: _____

# Mixed Review and Test Prep

**5** Which numbers describe the arrangement of cubes?

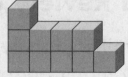

**A.** $5 + 4 + 1$     **C.** $1 + 8 + 1$

**B.** $3 + 5 + 2$     **D.** $6 + 2 + 2$

# That Makes Cents!

How many of each coin would you use to make the total amount?

**Family Connection**

Students have been recognizing coin values, counting money, and solving problems involving money. You can help your child with math by providing a few coins and asking him or her to tell the total value of the collection.

| Total Amount | | | | |
|---|---|---|---|---|
| ① 41¢ | | | | |
| ② 67¢ | | | | |
| ③ 33¢ | | | | |
| ④ 99¢ | | | | |
| ⑤ 84¢ | | | | |
| ⑥ 22¢ | | | | |
| ⑦ 78¢ | | | | |
| ⑧ 55¢ | | | | |
| ⑨ 16¢ | | | | |

# Mixed Review and Test Prep

⑩ In Emilio's family, there are 10 feet and 50 toes. How many people are in his family?

**A.** 6     **B.** 5     **C.** 4     **D.** 3

**Mathematical Thinking at Grade 3**

# Twice as Nice

Think doubles as you
solve each problem.

**1** There are 36 crayons
in one box of crayons.
How many crayons are in two boxes? _____

**2** There are 15 fish in one tank
and the same number in another tank.
How many fish are in both tanks? _____

**3** Tomás has two rows of tomato plants.
Each row has 43 plants. How many
tomato plants are in both rows altogether? _____

**4** There are 12 eggs in one full carton.
How many eggs are in two full cartons? _____

**5** There are 30 books on each shelf in
Mr. Woo's classroom. How many books
are on two shelves? _____

## Mixed Review and Test Prep

**6** Inga used only ⬡ blocks to
cover this shape. How many
trapezoid blocks did she use?

**A.** 3      **B.** 4      **C.** 5      **D.** 6

# Double the Money!

You can use coins to help you solve each problem.

**Family Connection**
Students are continuing to solve problems involving money. On this page, money amounts are either doubled or divided in half. You might want to make up more problems like the ones below for your child to solve.

**1** Each day, Marc earns 1 quarter, 1 dime, and 1 nickel for doing chores. How much money does he earn in two days? _____ ¢

**2** Isabel has 43¢ in her bank. Her brother, Josh, has the same amount in his bank. How much money do they have altogether? _____ ¢

**3** Russell and Kenji earned $1.50 for walking the neighbor's dog. They want to split the money evenly. How much money should they each get? _____ ¢

**4** Sumi has the same coins in each of her two pockets. Altogether she has 8 coins that total 60¢. What coins are in each of her pockets?

Pocket 1: _____

Pocket 2: _____

# Mixed Review and Test Prep

**5** There are 12 children at Jesse's party. Which group has enough prizes for each child to get one?

**A.** 8 puzzles    **B.** 6 rings    **C.** 4 horns    **D.** 3 whistles
     2 hats          3 puzzles     2 hats       3 balls
     2 balls         2 hats       4 rings      3 puzzles

Name _____  Date _____

# What's the Rule?

How do the things in the first group go together? Write the rule.

**1** Fits the rule

Does **not** fit the rule

Rule: _____

**2** Fits the rule

Does **not** fit the rule

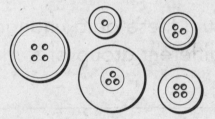

Rule: _____

# Mixed Review and Test Prep

**3** Solve this riddle.

I am the number of days in the week
plus the number of hours in one day.
What number am I?

**A.** 19          **B.** 24          **C.** 31          **D.** 33

**Mathematical Thinking at Grade 3**

# Displaying Data

**1** How could you group these students?
Make a graph to represent your data.

**Family Connection**

Students have been learning to collect, organize, and interpret data. On this page, they choose a way to group the children in the picture. Then they represent that data in a graph. You might want to ask your child to explain how he or she grouped the children.

*Be sure to write the category at the beginning of each row.*

|  |  |  |  |  |  |
|---|---|---|---|---|---|
|  |  |  |  |  |  |
|  |  |  |  |  |  |

**2** What information does this graph give you?

_____

_____

**3** Could these data change if we collected information from a different group of students? Why or why not?

_____

_____

# Mixed Review and Test Prep

**4** Leo, Mai, and Louis have a total of 15 pockets.
Which shows a way the children could be wearing 15 pockets altogether?

**A.** $10 + 8 + 1$    **C.** $7 + 3 + 5$

**B.** $9 + 2 + 5$    **D.** $6 + 5 + 2$

# Hefty Handfuls

Kenji wanted to know how many cubes he could hold in his hands. Here's how many he grabbed:

12 cubes                    18 cubes

**1** How many more cubes did Kenji grab with his right hand than with his left hand? _____

**2** How many cubes did Kenji grab altogether? _____

Olga grabbed 23 cubes with her left hand and 16 cubes with her right hand.

**3** How many more cubes did Olga grab with her left hand than with her right hand? _____

**4** How many cubes did Olga grab altogether? _____

## Mixed Review and Test Prep

**5** Juan brings 30 oranges for his class. There are 14 girls and 14 boys in his class. How many oranges are left over?

**A.** 0          **B.** 1          **C.** 2          **D.** 3

# A Fine Line

This line plot shows the number of cubes students in Ms. Martin's class can hold in their hands.

**Family Connection**

Students have been continuing to work with data. They have been learning to read and analyze data on a line plot. **Questions you might ask your child:** "How do you read a line plot? How do you know which numbers to put on the line plot?"

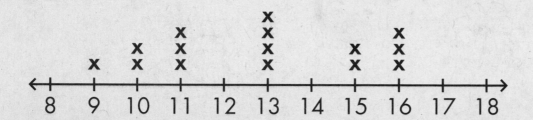

**1** What was the greatest number of cubes a student was able to hold? _____

**2** What was the least number of cubes a student held? _____

**3** How many cubes did the greatest number of students hold? _____

**4** How many more students held 13 cubes than held 15 cubes? _____

# Mixed Review and Test Prep

**5** Which shape shows a face of this block?

A.         B.         C.         D.

Name _____     Date _____

# Isn't That Odd?

Write an odd number in each △.

Write an even number in each □.

**Family Connection**

Students have been learning about odd and even numbers. On this page, students investigate adding odd and even numbers. You can help your child with math by saying a number and having him or her tell whether it is even or odd.

Is the sum **odd** or **even**?

**1** △ + △ = _____     _____

**2** □ + □ = _____     _____

**3** △ + □ = _____     _____

**4** When you added an odd number to an odd number, was the sum odd or even?     _____

**5** When you added an even number to an even number, was the sum odd or even?     _____

**6** When you added an odd number to an even number, was the sum odd or even?     _____

# Mixed Review and Test Prep

**7** Math class begins at 10:30 and lasts one hour. Which clock shows the time at which math class ends?

**A.**      **B.**      **C.**      **D.**

# Share with Me

Find out whether you need to use **halves** to solve the problem.

**Family Connection**

Students have been using calculators to solve problems involving dividing a number of items into two equal groups. They learned that sometimes they can split the items using whole numbers, but sometimes they must use halves. You might want to ask your child to explain how a calculator shows a half. (.5)

**1** Divide 14 grapes evenly between Jessica and Marcos. How many grapes does each child get? _____

Did you need to use halves? _____

**2** Divide 9 strawberries evenly between Eric and Anna. How many strawberries does each child get? _____

Did you need to use halves? _____

**3** Divide 11 bananas evenly between Lars and Carlos. How many bananas does each child get? _____

Did you need to use halves? _____

**4** Divide 8 pears evenly between Lina and Eiko. How many pears does each child get? _____

Did you need to use halves? _____

# Mixed Review and Test Prep

**5** Martha is playing a game on the 100 chart. She starts on 75, then moves forward 5. Next, she moves forward 15. What number is she on now?

**A.** 100     **B.** 95     **C.** 90     **D.** 85

Name _____                                Date _____

# Splitting Numbers

Write an even
number in the ☐.

Write an odd
number in the △.

**1** Split ☐ into two equal groups.
How many are in each group?                            _____

Did you need to use halves?                            _____

When you split the even number, did you
get an even number or an odd number?              _____
On another sheet of paper, tell why.

---

**2** Split △ into two equal groups.
How many are in each group?                            _____

Did you need to use halves?                            _____

When you split the odd number, did you
get an even number or an odd number?              _____
On another sheet of paper, tell why.

# Mixed Review and Test Prep

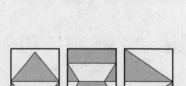

**3** Which card belongs in this group?

A.      B.      C.      D.

# Groups, Groups, Everywhere!

**Family Connection**

Students have been learning about things that come in groups. They have been writing and solving multiplication problems about groups. You might want to help your child look around the house or in the store for things that come in groups. Then ask him or her to tell how many come in two groups.

1. There are 4 wheels on a car.
   How many wheels are on 5 cars? _____

2. There are 2 wings on a bird.
   How many wings are on 6 birds? _____

3. There are 10 dimes in a dollar.
   How many dimes are in 4 dollars? _____

4. There are 7 days in a week.
   How many days are in 2 weeks? _____

5. There are 6 muffins in a box.
   How many muffins are in 5 boxes? _____

6. There are 8 legs on a spider.
   How many legs are on 3 spiders? _____

7. There are 12 months in a year.
   How many months are in 2 years? _____

## Mixed Review and Test Prep

8. Stefan has **more** than 10 toy animals in his collection. Which toy animals could be in his collection?

   **A.** 2 horses   **B.** 3 dogs   **C.** 4 cows   **D.** 5 cats
       2 cows       4 cats       3 horses       2 pigs
       6 pigs       3 horses       4 dogs       3 chickens

**Things That Come in Groups**

# Animal Groups

Write the multiplication sentence that goes with the picture.

**Family Connection**

Students continue to learn about equal groups and multiplication. They continue to explore solving problems and are learning to write multiplication number sentences. **Questions you might ask your child:** "Can you multiply if the groups are not equal?" "What does 3 × 2 mean?"

**1** 4 nests with 3 birds each

_____ × _____ = _____

**2** 3 dogs with 2 bones each

_____ × _____ = _____

**3** 5 ants with 6 legs each

_____ × _____ = _____

**4** 4 kittens with 4 paws each

_____ × _____ = _____

**5** 2 tanks with 7 fish each

_____ × _____ = _____

**6** 3 squirrels with 5 nuts each

_____ × _____ = _____

# Mixed Review and Test Prep

**7** Toshio has 15¢ in his pocket.
Which coins could **not** be his coins?

**A.** 10 pennies
1 nickel

**B.** 1 dime
2 nickels

**C.** 1 dime
1 nickel

**D.** 2 nickels
5 pennies

# Multiplication Match

**1** Match the problem to the solution.

**Family Connection**
Students continue to learn about multiplication. They have been drawing pictures of groups and making up riddles about multiplication situations. On this page, students find the missing parts of problems.

There are 4 children.
Each child saves 5 dimes.
How many dimes do they save in all?

There are 3 children.
Each child has the same number of balloons.
There are a total of 9 balloons.
How many balloons does each child have?

There are 5 children.
Each child has the same number of books.
Together they have 20 books.
How many books does each child have?

There are 5 children. Each child has 3 markers.
How many markers do they have altogether?

Each child has 3.

15 in all

20 in all

Each child has 4.

# Mixed Review and Test Prep

**2** Karen's first jump was 58 cubes long.
Her second jump was 36 cubes long.
How much longer was Karen's first jump?

**A.** 94 cubes   **B.** 58 cubes   **C.** 36 cubes   **D.** 22 cubes

**Things That Come in Groups**

# Multiple-Step Multiplication

Write the sentences that solve the problems.

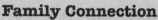
**1** 5 children were roller skating. Each child wore 2 skates. How many skates were there?

_____ × _____ = _____
children   skates      skates

Each skate had 4 rubber wheels. How many wheels were there?

_____ × _____ = _____
skates     wheels      wheels

**2** 3 dogs were digging holes. Each dog dug 3 holes. How many holes did they dig?

_____ × _____ = _____
dogs       holes       holes

The dogs buried 4 bones in each hole. How many bones did they bury?

_____ × _____ = _____
holes      bones       bones

## Mixed Review and Test Prep

**3** Lamar made half of a rectangle with blue tiles and the other half with red tiles. Which shows the numbers of tiles he used?

**A.** 3 blue
    4 red

**B.** 4 blue
    4 red

**C.** 5 blue
    4 red

**D.** 6 blue
    5 red

# Patterns of 2's and 3's

| 1 | 2 | 3 | 4 | 5 | 6 | 7 | 8 | 9 | 10 |
|---|---|---|---|---|---|---|---|---|----|
| 11 | 12 | 13 | 14 | 15 | 16 | 17 | 18 | 19 | 20 |
| 21 | 22 | 23 | 24 | 25 | 26 | 27 | 28 | 29 | 30 |
| 31 | 32 | 33 | 34 | 35 | 36 | 37 | 38 | 39 | 40 |
| 41 | 42 | 43 | 44 | 45 | 46 | 47 | 48 | 49 | 50 |
| 51 | 52 | 53 | 54 | 55 | 56 | 57 | 58 | 59 | 60 |
| 61 | 62 | 63 | 64 | 65 | 66 | 67 | 68 | 69 | 70 |
| 71 | 72 | 73 | 74 | 75 | 76 | 77 | 78 | 79 | 80 |
| 81 | 82 | 83 | 84 | 85 | 86 | 87 | 88 | 89 | 90 |
| 91 | 92 | 93 | 94 | 95 | 96 | 97 | 98 | 99 | 100 |

> **Family Connection**
>
> Students have been exploring multiples of 2 and 3 on a 100 chart. You can help your child with math by skip counting with him or her on the 100 chart. Start with 2 and count by 2's. Then start with 3 and count by 3's.
>
> **Questions you might ask your child:** "What patterns do the 2's make on the 100 chart?" "If I count by 3's on the 100 chart, will I say 15?"

Use the 100 chart to help you skip count.

**1** 2, 4, 6, _____, 10, 12, _____, 16, 18, _____, 22, _____, 26, 28, _____, 32, 34, _____, 38, 40, _____, _____, 46, 48, _____, 52, 54, 56, _____, 60, 62, 64, _____, _____

**2** 3, 6, 9, _____, 15, _____, 21, 24, 27, _____, 33, _____, 39, _____, 45, 48, _____, 54, 57, _____, _____, 66, 69, 72, 75, _____, _____, 84, _____, 90, _____, 96, 99

# Mixed Review and Test Prep

**3** Which shows a way to make 50?

**A.** 20 + 20 + 20 + 20          **C.** 15 + 5 + 15 + 5

**B.** 20 + 5 + 20 + 5          **D.** 10 + 10 + 10 + 10

**Things That Come in Groups**

# Calculator Patterns

| 1 | 2 | 3 | 4 | 5 | 6 | 7 | 8 | 9 | 10 |
|---|---|---|---|---|---|---|---|---|----|
| 11 | 12 | 13 | 14 | 15 | 16 | 17 | 18 | 19 | 20 |
| 21 | 22 | 23 | 24 | 25 | 26 | 27 | 28 | 29 | 30 |
| 31 | 32 | 33 | 34 | 35 | 36 | 37 | 38 | 39 | 40 |
| 41 | 42 | 43 | 44 | 45 | 46 | 47 | 48 | 49 | 50 |
| 51 | 52 | 53 | 54 | 55 | 56 | 57 | 58 | 59 | 60 |
| 61 | 62 | 63 | 64 | 65 | 66 | 67 | 68 | 69 | 70 |
| 71 | 72 | 73 | 74 | 75 | 76 | 77 | 78 | 79 | 80 |
| 81 | 82 | 83 | 84 | 85 | 86 | 87 | 88 | 89 | 90 |
| 91 | 92 | 93 | 94 | 95 | 96 | 97 | 98 | 99 | 100 |

**Family Connection**
Students continue to learn about patterns on a 100 chart and are exploring skip counting using a calculator. You can ask your child to explain how he or she uses the 100 chart and the calculator to skip count. This will help him or her clarify the mathematical ideas learned in class.

Write the number that would be displayed in the calculator window.

**1** ⓪ ➕ ④ ＝ ＝ ＝ ＝ ＝          _____

**2** ⓪ ➕ ③ ＝ ＝ ＝ ＝          _____

**3** ⓪ ➕ ⑤ ＝ ＝ ＝ ＝ ＝          _____

**4** ⓪ ➕ ⑩ ＝ ＝ ＝ ＝ ＝ ＝          _____

**5** ⓪ ➕ ⑥ ＝ ＝ ＝ ＝          _____

## Mixed Review and Test Prep

**6** On the last Pocket Day, there were 45 pockets. How many more pockets are there today?

**A.** 7          **B.** 8          **C.** 14          **D.** 21

**Today's Pockets**

52

**Things That Come in Groups**

# Skip-Counting Patterns

| 1 | 2 | 3 | 4 | 5 | 6 | 7 | 8 | 9 | 10 |
|---|---|---|---|---|---|---|---|---|----|
| 11 | 12 | 13 | 14 | 15 | 16 | 17 | 18 | 19 | 20 |
| 21 | 22 | 23 | 24 | 25 | 26 | 27 | 28 | 29 | 30 |
| 31 | 32 | 33 | 34 | 35 | 36 | 37 | 38 | 39 | 40 |
| 41 | 42 | 43 | 44 | 45 | 46 | 47 | 48 | 49 | 50 |
| 51 | 52 | 53 | 54 | 55 | 56 | 57 | 58 | 59 | 60 |
| 61 | 62 | 63 | 64 | 65 | 66 | 67 | 68 | 69 | 70 |
| 71 | 72 | 73 | 74 | 75 | 76 | 77 | 78 | 79 | 80 |
| 81 | 82 | 83 | 84 | 85 | 86 | 87 | 88 | 89 | 90 |
| 91 | 92 | 93 | 94 | 95 | 96 | 97 | 98 | 99 | 100 |

You can use the 100 chart to help.

## Skip count forward or backward.

**1** 22, 24, 26, _____, 30, _____, 34, 36, _____, _____

**2** 100, 95, 90, _____, 80, 75, _____, _____, 60, _____

**3** 39, 42, 45, 48, _____, _____, 57, _____, 63, _____, 69

**4** 100, 90, 80, _____, _____, 50, 40, _____, _____, 10

**5** 48, 52, 56, 60, _____, 68, _____, 76, _____, 84, _____

# Mixed Review and Test Prep

**6** Nora's desktop measures 6 blue paper strips in length. Yellow paper strips are half as long as blue strips. How many yellow strips long is Nora's desk?

**A.** 12      **B.** 8      **C.** 4      **D.** 3

**Things That Come in Groups**

# How Many Towers?

Color the towers to help you solve the problem.

**Family Connection**

Students continue to work with multiplication concepts. They have been using interlocking cubes to solve problems about multiples and have been learning to write multiplication sentences. You can help your child with math by having him or her do simple skip counting for you, such as 2, 4, 6, 8, and so on.

**1** How many 3's are there in 36?

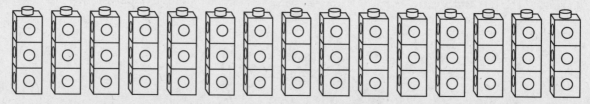

$$3 \times \underline{\hspace{1cm}} = 36$$

**2** How many 5's are there in 55?

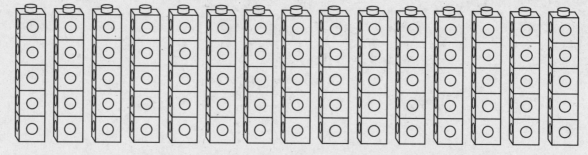

$$5 \times \underline{\hspace{1cm}} = 55$$

# Mixed Review and Test Prep

**3** Rachel earned 50¢ for pulling weeds and 35¢ for washing the car. When she has $1, she can buy a book at the school store. How much more money does she need?

**A.** 10¢          **B.** 15¢          **C.** 20¢          **D.** 25¢

**Things That Come in Groups**

# Riddle Me This!

**1** Which animal likes to play baseball?

To find out, connect the multiples of 9. Then connect the multiples of 11.

**Family Connection**

Students continue to learn about multiples and multiplication. As they skip count the multiples for a given number, they are learning about multiplying groups of that number. For example, saying 2, 4, 6, 8 is a way of finding $2 \times 4$. On this page, students connect the dots for the multiples of 9 and the multiples of 11 to answer the riddle.

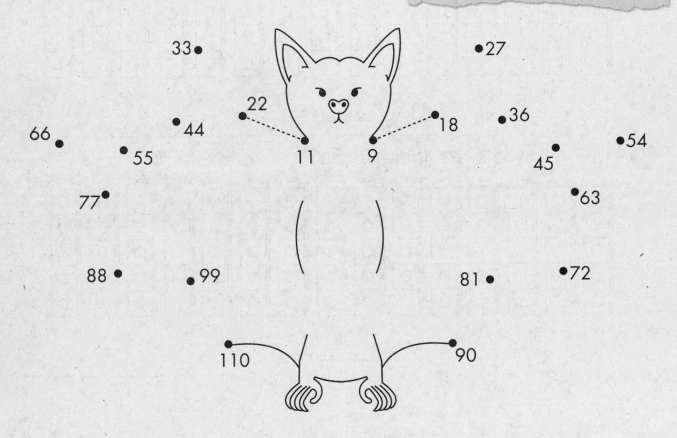

# Mixed Review and Test Prep

**2** Together, Rosa, Jim, and Ping collected 100 seashells. Rosa found 28. Jim found 42. How many did Ping find?

**A.** 14  **B.** 24  **C.** 30  **D.** 40

**Things That Come in Groups**

# Mystery Multiples

| 1 | 2 | 3 | 4 | 5 | 6 | 7 | 8 | 9 | 10 |
|---|---|---|---|---|---|---|---|---|---|
| 11 | 12 | 13 | 14 | 15 | 16 | 17 | 18 | 19 | 20 |
| 21 | 22 | 23 | 24 | 25 | 26 | 27 | 28 | 29 | 30 |
| 31 | 32 | 33 | 34 | 35 | 36 | 37 | 38 | 39 | 40 |
| 41 | 42 | 43 | 44 | 45 | 46 | 47 | 48 | 49 | 50 |
| 51 | 52 | 53 | 54 | 55 | 56 | 57 | 58 | 59 | 60 |
| 61 | 62 | 63 | 64 | 65 | 66 | 67 | 68 | 69 | 70 |
| 71 | 72 | 73 | 74 | 75 | 76 | 77 | 78 | 79 | 80 |
| 81 | 82 | 83 | 84 | 85 | 86 | 87 | 88 | 89 | 90 |
| 91 | 92 | 93 | 94 | 95 | 96 | 97 | 98 | 99 | 100 |

**Family Connection**

Students have been comparing the patterns of multiples in numbers 2 through 12 on 100 charts. They have discovered that some sets of multiples are all even numbers, and some sets of multiples are on more than one chart. For example, all the multiples of 4 are also multiples of 2. **Questions you might ask your child:** "Which multiple charts have some of the same multiples on them?" "Which numbers are not multiples of 2?"

**1** What are some multiples of 10?

_____, _____, _____, _____, _____, _____

What other numbers have these multiples highlighted on their skip-count charts?     _____ and _____

**2** What are some multiples of 6?

_____, _____, _____, _____, _____, _____

What other numbers have these multiples highlighted on their skip-count charts?     _____ and _____

# Mixed Review and Test Prep

**3** Max took a survey to see how many pieces of pizza students ate for dinner. How many pieces did the students eat altogether?

**Pizza Pieces We Ate**

| 1 | ✓ ✓ ✓ ✓ ✓ ✓ ✓ ✓ |
|---|---|
| 2 | ✓ ✓ ✓ ✓ |
| 3 | ✓ ✓ |

**A.** 30          **B.** 23          **C.** 15          **D.** 9

**Things That Come in Groups**

# Sizing Up Arrays

Write the dimensions of each rectangle.

**Family Connection**

Students have been working with arrays, rectangles made out of items placed in equal rows. They have been learning that the dimensions of an array describe its length and width (or height). **Questions you might ask your child:** "How do you find the dimensions of each array?" "Do you have to have the same number of squares in each row to make an array?"

**1**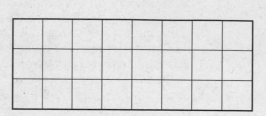

_____ × _____

**2**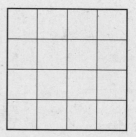

_____ × _____

**3**

_____ × _____

**4**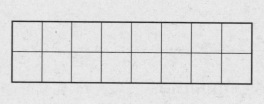

_____ × _____

**5**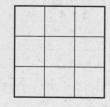

_____ × _____

# Mixed Review and Test Prep

**6** Bernard made groups of 5 to count the cubes in a bag. He had no cubes left over. Which could **not** have been the number of cubes he counted?

**A.** 47  **B.** 35  **C.** 20  **D.** 15

**Things That Come in Groups**

# Shammi's Garden

Shammi is planting a garden.
Find a way to plant the seeds in
equal rows. Draw each way and
write the dimensions.

**Family Connection**

Students have been learning
that when items are placed in
equal rows, they form an array.
An array can be described with
multiplication. For example,
3 rows of 4 items forms an
array that has the dimensions
of 3 by 4 or 3 × 4.

**1** 16 carrot seeds

_____ × _____

**2** 24 pepper seeds

_____ × _____

**3** 15 tomato seeds

___ × ____

**4** 20 watermelon seeds

___ × ____

# Mixed Review and Test Prep

**5** Therese made up the following pattern:
**Clap, clap, turn around, clap, clap, turn around.**
Which shows the same pattern using symbols?

A. ☆☺☆☺☆☺

C. ✿✿❀✿✿❀

B. ⊘♡♡⊘♡♡

D. ⊘⊘⊘○○○

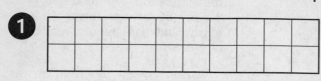

**Things That Come in Groups**

# Tell Me the Total!

Write the dimensions of each array.
Then write the total number of squares.

**Family Connection**
Students continue to learn about multiplication through the use of arrays. On this page, they find the dimensions of each array (length and height) and then find the total number of squares in the array. The total can be found by multiplying or skip counting. Ask your child to explain how he or she found the total for each of these arrays.

**1**

\_\_\_\_\_ × \_\_\_\_\_

Total squares \_\_\_\_\_

**2**

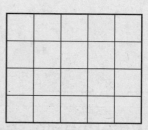

\_\_\_\_\_ × \_\_\_\_\_

Total squares \_\_\_\_\_

**3**

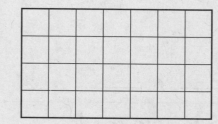

\_\_\_\_\_ × \_\_\_\_\_

Total squares \_\_\_\_\_

**4**

\_\_\_\_\_ × \_\_\_\_\_

Total squares \_\_\_\_\_

**5**

\_\_\_\_\_ × \_\_\_\_\_

Total squares \_\_\_\_\_

# Mixed Review and Test Prep

**6** $30 - 12 = \boxed{\phantom{xx}}$

**A.** 30      **B.** 28      **C.** 18      **D.** 12

**Things That Come in Groups**

# Which Is Larger?

Write an **X** on the array you think is larger. Then find the total squares in each. Circle the array that really is larger.

**1**

$2 \times 8$

$3 \times 3$

Total squares _____          Total squares _____

**2**

$4 \times 4$

$3 \times 5$

Total squares _____          Total squares _____

**3**
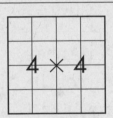

$3 \times 8$

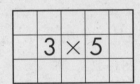

$4 \times 7$

Total squares _____          Total squares _____

# Mixed Review and Test Prep

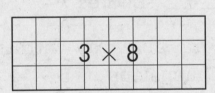**4** Lori used two coupons that saved her $1 after they were doubled. Which could be the values of Lori's coupons?

    **A.** 15¢ and 25¢   **C.** 50¢ and 45¢

    **B.** 20¢ and 30¢   **D.** 65¢ and 25¢

# Rectangle Riddles

Can you solve these
rectangle riddles?

**Family Connection**

Students continue to learn about factors in
multiplication by exploring the relationship between
an array's dimensions and its total number of
squares. On this page, students are given 2 out of
the 3 measurements for an array and must determine
the missing measurement.

**1** I am an array with the
dimensions of 4 × 4.
How many squares do
I have in all?

_____ squares

**2** I am an array with
12 squares in all.
My length is 6 squares.
What is my height?

_____ squares

**3** I am an array with the
dimensions of 3 × 6.
How many squares do
I have in all?

_____ squares

**4** I am an array with
15 squares in all.
My length is 5 squares.
What is my height?

_____ squares

**5** I am an array with a
height of 2 squares.
I have 16 squares in all.
What is my length?

_____ squares

**6** I am an array with the
dimensions of 5 × 4.
How many squares do
I have in all?

_____ squares

# Mixed Review and Test Prep

**7** How many cubes would
there be in 10 towers?

**A.** 110  **B.** 100  **C.** 95  **D.** 90

**Things That Come in Groups**

# Multiply or Divide?

**Family Connection**
Students have been learning about the relationship between multiplication and division. On this page, students chose a way to solve each problem and then decided whether they used multiplication or division.

What **will** you do?

**1** Zoe and Yuki have a bag of 30 pretzels.
They want to share them evenly.
How many pretzels should each girl get? _____

Did you multiply or divide? _____

**2** Webster has 5 boxes of granola bars for
his class. Each box has 6 granola bars.
How many granola bars are there altogether? _____

Did you multiply or divide? _____

**3** Latisha picks 24 flowers from her garden.
She wants to put the same number of flowers
in each of three vases. How many flowers
should she put in each vase? _____

Did you multiply or divide? _____

## Mixed Review and Test Prep

**4** Mario collected a button, a penny,
an egg, a counter, and a small ball.
What is the same about all these things?

**A.** You can eat them.

**C.** They are all big things.

**B.** They have round parts.

**D.** They have straight sides.

**Things That Come in Groups**

# Match Me Up!

**1** Match the picture to the problems. Then solve all of the problems!

**Family Connection**

Students continue to learn about the relationship between multiplication and division. **Questions you might ask your child:** "How does each picture show division?" "How does each picture show multiplication?"

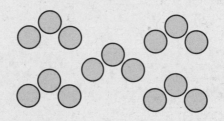

How many 4's in 20? _____

$20 \div 4 =$ _____

5 groups of 4 are _____ altogether.

$5 \times 4 =$ _____

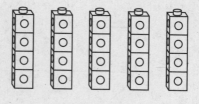

5 groups of 6 are _____ altogether.

$5 \times 6 =$ _____

How many 6's in 30? _____

$30 \div 6 =$ _____

How many 3's in 15? _____

$15 \div 3 =$ _____

5 groups of 3 are _____ altogether.

$5 \times 3 =$ _____

# Mixed Review and Test Prep

**2** There are 24 students in Mr. Levine's class. Which could be the number of boys and girls in his class?

**A.** 16 boys and 15 girls    **C.** 14 boys and 14 girls

**B.** 15 boys and 13 girls    **D.** 12 boys and 12 girls

# How Many?

Write a multiplication or division
sentence to solve the problem.

**Family Connection**
Students have been writing
their own multiplication
and division problems.
They made a class book of
all the problems and are
working on solving each
one. Ask your child to
explain each of the
problems on this page. This
will help your child clarify
his or her thinking around
multiplication and division
concepts.

**1** Mrs. Moy bought 4 packages of
juice boxes. Each package had
6 boxes of juice in it. How many
boxes of juice is that in all?

_____ boxes of juice

**2** Sara has 18 trading cards that she wants
to share with her two friends. Each child,
including Sara, gets the same number of cards.
How many trading cards will each child get?

_____ trading cards

**3** Alfonso has 7 corn plants.
Each corn plant has 5 ears of corn on it.
How many ears of corn does Alfonso
have on all his plants?

_____ ears of corn

## Mixed Review and Test Prep

**4** In Kira's class, today's number is 34.
Which does **not** show a way to make 34?

**A.** 15 + 16    **B.** 17 + 17    **C.** 46 − 12    **D.** 60 − 26

**Things That Come in Groups**

# Two-Part Problems

Write multiplication or division sentences to solve these two-part problems.

**Family Connection**

Students continue to write and solve their own multiplication and division problems. On this page, all of the problems involve two steps, and so children write two number sentences to solve them.

**1** Matthew has 30 boxes of raisins. He shares them equally with the children at his lunch table. There are 6 children altogether. There are 10 raisins in each box. How many raisins does each child get?

_____ boxes per child

_____ raisins per child

**2** Jamal has 2 cats. Each cat has 4 kittens. Each kitten has 3 toys. How many toys do the kittens have altogether?

_____ kittens

_____ toys

# Mixed Review and Test Prep

**3** There are 26 children in Mrs. Ramirez's class.
There are 32 children in Mr. Becker's class.
How many more children are in Mr. Becker's class?

**A.** 16        **B.** 8        **C.** 6        **D.** 5

# Smart Savings

How much money could you save
in 1 year? What could you buy
with that money?

**Family Connection**
Students have been solving
problems about saving money. You
can help your child with math by
talking to him or her about how to
read the table on this page. Also,
you might want to ask your child
if he or she sees any patterns in
the table.

| | If I save this much each month ... | I will save this much in 1 year! | This is what I could buy at the end of 1 year: |
|---|---|---|---|
| 1 | $1 | | |
| 2 | $2 | | |
| 3 | $3 | | |
| 4 | $4 | | |
| 5 | $5 | | |
| 6 | $6 | | |
| 7 | $7 | | |
| 8 | $8 | | |

# Mixed Review and Test Prep

9 If each letter is worth 5¢, how much money is
the name **Maurice** worth?

   A. 30¢         B. 35¢         C. 40¢         D. 45¢

10 How much money is the name **Janice** worth?

   A. 30¢         B. 35¢         C. 40¢         D. 45¢

# Spots and Stripes

Solve each problem.

**1** This butterfly has
6 spots on each wing.
How many spots are on
5 butterflies like this one? _____

**2** This fish has 5 stripes.
How many stripes are on
8 fish like this one? _____

**3** This frog has 7 spots.
How many spots are on
10 frogs like this one? _____

**4** This zebra has 9 stripes.
How many stripes are on
3 zebras like this one? _____

**5** This ladybug has 4 spots.
How many spots are on
7 ladybugs like this one? _____

# Mixed Review and Test Prep

**6** Which animal swims and flies?

A. bat

B. whale

C. duck

D. fish

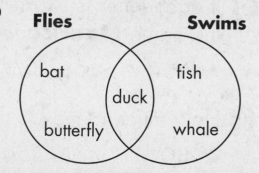

Flies          Swims

bat    duck    fish

butterfly    whale

**Things That Come in Groups**

## Pet Data

This line plot shows
data about how many
pets the students in
Sabrina's class have.

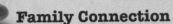

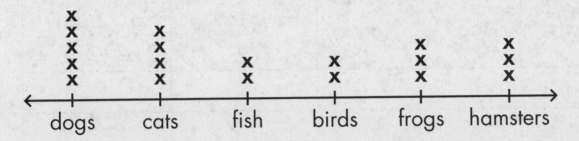

**1** How many eyes are there on all the pets altogether?  _____

**2** How many legs are there on all the dogs and
all the cats together?                                    _____

**3** Frogs have 4 legs and birds have 2 legs.
How many legs are on all the frogs
and birds together?                                      _____

**4** Write your own question about the data on the line plot.

_____

_____

## Mixed Review and Test Prep

**5** 70 − 63 = ☐

**A.** 2          **B.** 6          **C.** 7          **D.** 8

# 12 Eyes and 12 Ears

Shawna has cats, dogs, and horses. Her pets have a total of 12 eyes and 12 ears. How many of each kind of pet could she have?

**Family Connection**

Students continue to solve problems involving multiplication and division. **Questions you might ask your child:** "How did you decide how many of each pet Shawna could have?" "What patterns do you see in the table?"

| | Cats | Dogs | Horses | How many eyes? | How many ears? |
|---|---|---|---|---|---|
| 1 | 4 | 1 | 1 | 12 | 12 |
| 2 | | | | | |
| 3 | | | | | |
| 4 | | | | | |
| 5 | | | | | |
| 6 | | | | | |
| 7 | | | | | |
| 8 | | | | | |
| 9 | | | | | |
| 10 | | | | | |

# Mixed Review and Test Prep

**1** Which shape **can** be cut into identical halves in only one way?

A.     B.     C.     D. ▭

**Flips, Turns, and Area**

# Match the Shapes

Color the tetromino on the right that is the **same shape** as the one on the left.

**Family Connection**

Students have been working with tetrominoes (shapes made with 4 squares). They have discovered that there are 5 different tetrominoes and that tetrominoes of the same size and shape can be flipped and turned to fit on top of each other.

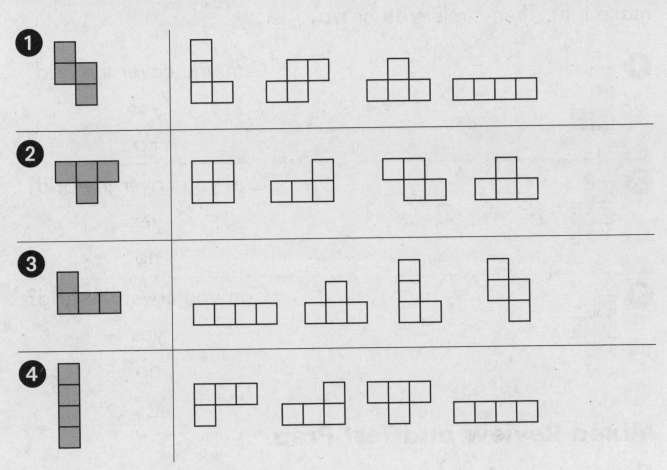

1

2

3

4

# Mixed Review and Test Prep

5 Strip A is half as long as Strip B. Strip C is twice as long as Strip B. Which object is twice as long as the eraser?

| Strip A | Strip B | Strip C |
|---------|---------|---------|
| crayon scissors | glue eraser | book tablet |

**A.** scissors     **B.** book     **C.** glue     **D.** crayon

# Copycat

Can you cover the grid with the tetromino? Copy the tetromino onto the grid as many times as you can. Slide, flip, and turn the shape to make it fit. Then circle **yes** or **no**.

1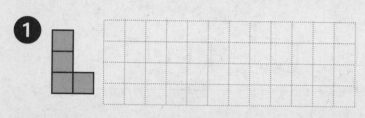

Can you cover the grid?

yes

no

2

Can you cover the grid?

yes

no

3

Can you cover the grid?

yes

no

# Mixed Review and Test Prep

4 Tanesha made the following timeline to show her class schedule. Which two times are missing?

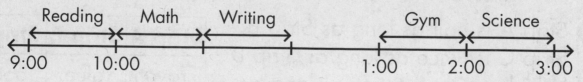

**A.** 8:00 and 11:30     **C.** 11:00 and 12:00

**B.** 9:00 and 1:00     **D.** 1:30 and 4:00

# It's Your Move

How was each tetromino moved? Circle **slide, turn,** or **flip.**

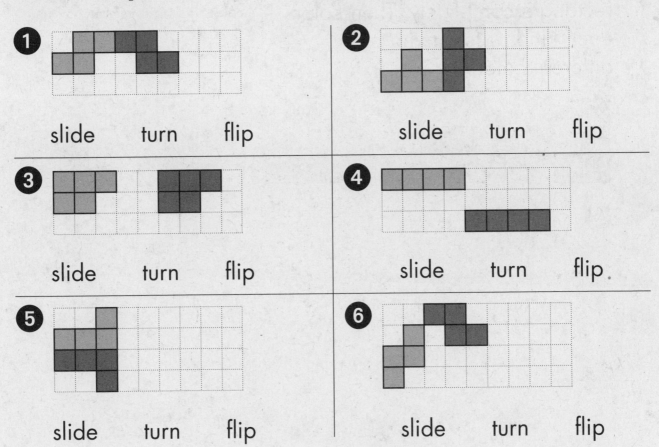

**1**      slide      turn      flip

**2**      slide      turn      flip

**3**      slide      turn      flip

**4**      slide      turn      flip

**5**      slide      turn      flip

**6**      slide      turn      flip

# Mixed Review and Test Prep

**7** You need only 15¢ more to have $1.
Which coins might you have?

**A.** 3 quarters
2 dimes
1 nickel

**B.** 2 quarters
3 dimes
4 nickels

**C.** 1 quarter
5 dimes
2 nickels

**D.** 1 quarter
2 dimes
6 nickels

# Cover Me

**1** Use a pencil to draw tetrominoes on the grid. Use some of each tetromino shape and cover the rectangle completely. Then color each kind of tetromino a different color.

**Family Connection**
Students continue to explore 2-D geometry by covering rectangles with tetrominoes. **Questions you might ask your child:** "How is this rectangle different from others you have covered with tetrominoes? How is it the same? Are there other ways to cover this rectangle?"

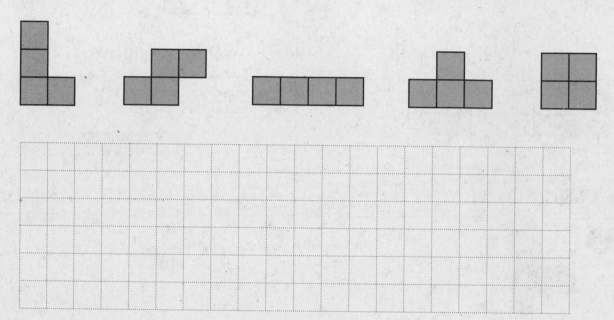

# Mixed Review and Test Prep

**2** You might see this number on a calculator. What does it mean?

$12.16$

**A.** a little more than 12

**B.** a little less than 12

**C.** a little less than 120

**D.** a little less than 1200

**Flips, Turns, and Area**

# The Perfect Fit

**1** Draw a line from each hole in the puzzle to the piece that will fit there exactly. You can turn pieces, but do **not** flip them!

# Mixed Review and Test Prep

**2** There are 27 students in Lea's class. 14 wear glasses. How many do not?

**A.** 11          **C.** 23

**B.** 13          **D.** 41

**Interesting Tidbit**

The first jigsaw puzzles were made in 1760 out of wooden maps cut into small pieces. Today, the largest jigsaw puzzle has more than 18,000 pieces and measures more than 9 feet by 6 feet!

**Flips, Turns, and Area**

# How Many Squares?

How many square units are in
each rectangle? How many
square units are covered?
Do **not** count one-by-one!

**Family Connection**

Students have been exploring the
concept of area by covering
rectangles with smaller shapes.
The shapes used on this page are
all tetrominoes (shapes made of
4 squares). Ask your child to
explain how he or she found the
number of square units that are
covered on each rectangle.

**1**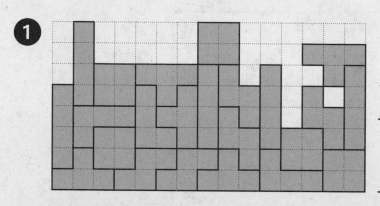

_____ square units in the
        whole rectangle

_____ square units covered

**2**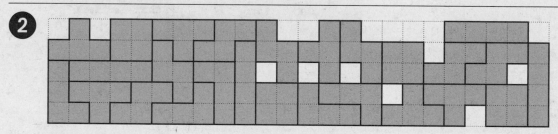

_____ square units in the whole rectangle

_____ square units covered

# Mixed Review and Test Prep

**3** How many of the shaded triangle
would it take to cover the
larger shape?

  **A.** 12        **C.** 8

  **B.** 10       **D.** 6

Name _____  Date _____

# Color Four

Color more spaces to make each shape have an area of 4 square units. REMEMBER: Each shape must have full sides touching.

**Family Connection**

Students continue to explore area. Each shape on this page should have an area of 4 square units. **Questions you might ask your child:** "If each square is one square unit, how much space does one triangle cover?" "How did you decide how much to color on each shape?"

①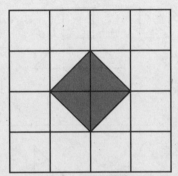

②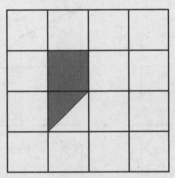

③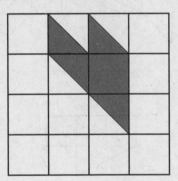

④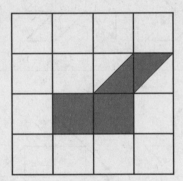

# Mixed Review and Test Prep

⑤ Mrs. Hill has 24 pencils. There are 12 boys and 14 girls in the class. How many more pencils does Mrs. Hill need for each student to get one?

**A.** 1 more      **B.** 2 more      **C.** 3 more      **D.** 4 more

# Same or Different?

Which pairs of shapes are congruent?
Could you turn and/or flip the shapes
to fit exactly on top of each other?
Draw a circle around each pair of
shapes that match exactly.

**Family Connection**

Students have been working with
the idea of congruence. Figures are
congruent if they are exactly the
same size and shape. **Questions
you might ask your child:** "How
would this shape have to be moved
in order to fit it exactly on top of
the other shape? Would you flip
it? Would you turn it?"

**1**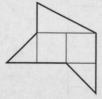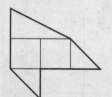

**2**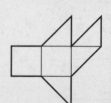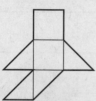

**3**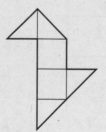

**4**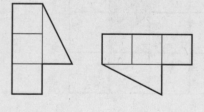

**5**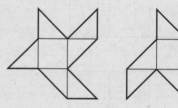

**6**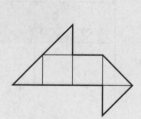

# Mixed Review and Test Prep

**7** You want to move from 54 to 76 on the 100 chart.
Which number string shows a way you could do it?

**A.** $54 + 30 + 2 + 10$          **C.** $54 + 20 - 2 + 10$

**B.** $54 - 30 + 2 - 10$          **D.** $54 + 10 + 2 + 10$

# Exactly Six!

Draw a different shape on each dot grid. Each shape has to have an area of 6 square units.

**1** Use only squares.

. . . . . .

. . . . . .

. . . . . .

. . . . . .

**2** Use only triangles.

. . . . . .

. . . . . .

. . . . . .

. . . . . .

# Mixed Review and Test Prep

**3** 14 students were surveyed to find out how many teeth they had lost. The greatest number of students lost 8 teeth. Which line plot could show the data?

A.
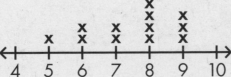

C.
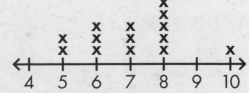

B.
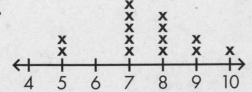

D.
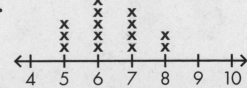

**Flips, Turns, and Area**

# Strictly Seven!

Draw a different shape on each dot grid. Each shape has to have an area of 7 square units.

**Family Connection**

Students are continuing to explore the idea of the areas of shapes. On this page, students draw shapes having an area of 7 square units. **Questions you might ask your child:** "How could you change the shape in Exercise 1 so that it has 8 square units?" "How could you change the shape in Exercise 2 so that it has 6 square units?"

**1** Use only squares.

. . . . . . .
. . . . . . .
. . . . . . .
. . . . . . .
. . . . . . .

**2** Use only triangles.

. . . . . . .
. . . . . . .
. . . . . . .
. . . . . . .
. . . . . . .

# Mixed Review and Test Prep

**3** Sergio cut 3 symmetrical shapes out of folded paper. Which shape is **not** Sergio's?

A.

B.

C.

D.

**From Paces to Feet**

# Giant Steps

This line plot shows how many giant steps students in Room 222 took to walk the length of their classroom.

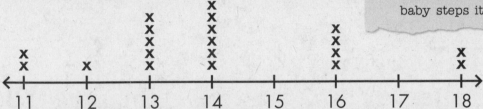

**1** How many students participated in the survey? _____

**2** How many giant steps did the most students take? _____

**3** What were the fewest giant steps taken to walk the length of the classroom? _____

**4** What were the most giant steps taken to walk the length of the classroom? _____

**5** Why do you think students took different numbers of giant steps to cover the same distance?

_____

_____

# Mixed Review and Test Prep

**6** $26 + 12 = \boxed{\phantom{00}}$

A. 14　　　　　C. 38

B. 28　　　　　D. 40

**From Paces to Feet**

# Comparing Steps

These line plots show how many giant steps, baby steps, and paces it took some students in Room 222 to walk the length of the hallway.

**Family Connection**

Students continue to measure distances using different-sized steps. They have been interpreting and comparing data sets. **Questions you might ask your child:** "Which are the largest steps? Which are the smallest? Do you need to take more giant steps or more baby steps?"

giant steps          baby steps          paces

**1** What were the most of each kind of step taken?

_____    _____    _____
giant steps    baby steps    paces

**2** What were the fewest of each kind of step taken?

_____    _____    _____
giant steps    baby steps    paces

**3** Why do you think the data for each of the steps are so different? _____

_____

# Mixed Review and Test Prep

**4** Pete's Tropical Fish Store has a total of 98 fish in two tanks. How many fish could be in the tanks?

**A.** 76 and 34          **C.** 57 and 21

**B.** 66 and 32          **D.** 44 and 14

Name _____    Date _____

# Giving Directions

Olga Kiel made this map of the office space where her dad works. Each square is a step.

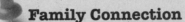

**Family Connection**

Students have been learning to give "robot" directions to help someone get from one point to another within the school. They took turns being the direction-giver or the robot. They have been estimating the distances in numbers of paces and then checking to see how close their estimates were.

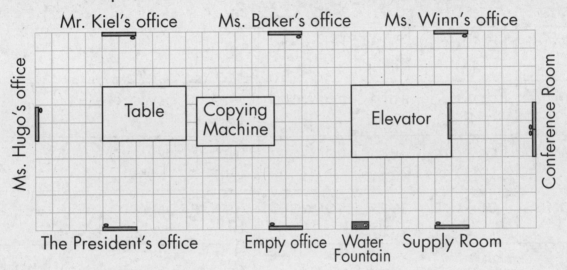

Write robot directions for each route.

**1** Going from Mr. Kiel's door to the copying machine

_____

_____

**2** Going from the elevator door to Mr. Kiel's door

_____

_____

# Mixed Review and Test Prep

**3** The sum of these numbers is 75.

**A.** 10, 20, 15   **B.** 15, 20, 20   **C.** 25, 20, 15   **D.** 25, 25, 25

Name _____  Date _____

# Show Me the Way

**1** Write the total number of paces for each student's route.

| Name | Route from Room 222 to the Gym | | | | | Total Paces |
|------|---------|------------|------------|-----------|------------|-------------|
| Su-Mei | Forward 10 | Turn Right | Forward 8 | Turn Left | Forward 6 | |
| Tom | Forward 8 | Turn Right | Forward 8 | Turn Left | Forward 10 | |
| Lee | Forward 10 | Turn Right | Forward 8 | Turn Left | Forward 2 | |
| Maria | Forward 2 | Turn Right | Forward 12 | Turn Left | Forward 16 | |

**2** Whose route is the shortest? _____

**3** Whose route is the longest? _____

**4** Why do you think one route might be longer

than another? _____

_____

# Mixed Review and Test Prep

**5** How many more students wore shirts with pictures than wore plain shirts?

A. 9          C. 5

B. 7          D. 3

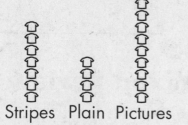

Stripes  Plain  Pictures

**From Paces to Feet**

# The Middle-Sized Pace Length

The class decided that Christy had the middle-sized pace.

**Pace Lengths**

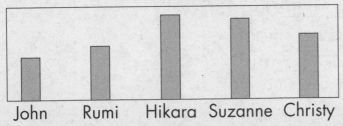

John    Rumi    Hikara    Suzanne    Christy

**Family Connection**
Students have been determining the sizes of their own paces and then deciding which pace in the class is the middle-sized pace. They have been measuring distances using the middle-sized pace and also using their own paces. You might want to invite your child to show you how he or she can measure the length or width of a room using paces.

**1** Why do you think Christy's pace length was chosen?

_____

_____

**2** The length of the classroom measured 10 of Christy's paces. Would it take **more or fewer than 10** of John's paces to measure the same distance? Explain why.

_____

_____

## Mixed Review and Test Prep

**3** Which set of cards has a sum that is closest to 20?

A.      B.     C.     D. 6 8 7

© Pearson Education, Inc. 3

**From Paces to Feet**

# Pace Problems

Use the standard-pace tape at the right. Find starting and ending points that have the given distance between them. (HINT: Your measurements do not have to be exact.)

**Family Connection**

Students have been using a standard-pace tape to measure distances. They are beginning to discover that without a standard unit, measurements can vary considerably. Ask your child to explain how his or her class determined the size for the standard-pace tape.

**1** About 5 standard paces:

_____          _____

     starting point                      ending point

**2** About 8 standard paces:

_____          _____

     starting point                      ending point

**3** About 10 standard paces:

_____          _____

     starting point                      ending point

**4** About 15 standard paces:

_____          _____

     starting point                      ending point

Standard-pace tape

# Mixed Review and Test Prep

**5** Double 12. Then double 6. What is the sum of these two numbers?

**A.** 18       **B.** 24       **C.** 30       **D.** 36

**From Paces to Feet**

# Inch By Inch

**1** Use a ruler to measure the length of your hand from the tip of your longest finger to your wrist.

My hand is about _____ inches long.

**2** How did you use the ruler to measure your hand?

_____

_____

**3** What might make the measurement change if you measure your hand again?

_____

_____

**4** Find someone with a longer hand. Write this person's ...

name: _____     age: _____

length of hand: _____ inches

## Mixed Review and Test Prep

**5** Four ◇ cover the shape at the right. How many ▷ will cover the shape?

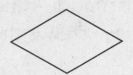

**A.** 12          **B.** 8          **C.** 6          **D.** 4

# Foot Findings

Colin measured the length of every teacher's foot to the nearest inch. Here are the data:

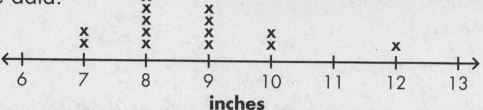

inches

**1** How long was the longest foot measured? _____

**2** What was the typical length for all the feet measured? _____

**3** Why do you think this is so?

_____

_____

**4** How many teachers work at Colin's school? _____

# Mixed Review and Test Prep

**5** The chart at the right shows how old students were on the first day of school. After 5 children had birthdays, the class made a new chart. Which chart below shows the new data?

**Our Ages**

| 8 | ＨＴＩＩＩ |
|---|---|
| 9 | ＨＴＩ |
| 10 | ＩＩＩＩ |

**A.**

| 8 | ＩＩＩ |
|---|---|
| 9 | ＨＴＩ |
| 10 | ＩＩＩＩ |

**B.**

| 8 | ＩＩＩ |
|---|---|
| 9 | ＨＴＨＴ |
| 10 | ＩＩＩＩ |

**C.**

| 8 | ＨＴＩＩＩ |
|---|---|
| 9 | ＨＴＩＩＩ |
| 10 | ＨＴＩ |

**D.**

| 8 | ＨＴＩＩＩ |
|---|---|
| 9 | ＨＴＨＴＩ |
| 10 | ＩＩＩＩ |

Name _____    Date _____

# Measure This!

Find each object, measure it with a ruler, and record the measurement. Circle the taller or longer object in each row.

**Family Connection**

Students have been measuring and comparing the lengths and widths of objects using inches. You can help your child by encouraging him or her to measure things around the house and then to compare pairs of objects to find out which object is longer or shorter. (If you don't have one of the objects pictured on this page, substitute something similar.)

**1** 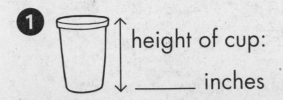 height of cup: _____ inches      height of can: _____ inches

**2** length of a spoon: _____ inches       width of a plate: _____ inches

**3** length of a crayon: _____ inches      length of a pen: _____ inches

**4** Measure the lengths of two other objects. On another sheet of paper, draw the objects and write the measurements. Circle the longer object.

## Mixed Review and Test Prep

**5** There are 13 girls, 15 boys, and 30 balloons. If each student gets a balloon, how many balloons will be left over?

**A.** 1          **B.** 2          **C.** 12          **D.** 15

Name _____                     Date _____

# Plotting Jumps

The students in Room 222 measured how far they could jump.

| How Far We Jumped in Inches | | | | | |
|---|---|---|---|---|---|
| Jackie | 22 | Lila | 18 | Jesse | 24 |
| Rosa | 18 | Jozef | 23 | Lidie | 23 |
| Adam | 26 | Shawna | 21 | Nicole | 22 |
| Martin | 20 | Ira | 22 | Michael | 22 |

**1** Use the data to make a line plot. Mark an **X** above the line for each measurement.

18  19  20  21  22  23  24  25  26

**inches**

**2** What was the range from the shortest jump to the longest jump?

_____ inches to _____ inches

**3** How long is a typical jump for this class? _____ inches

**4** Why do you think this is so?

**Interesting Tidbit**

Before the 2004 Olympic games, the record long jump for a man was 29 feet, 4.5 inches. The record long jump for a woman was 24 feet, 8 inches. Were the records broken?

---

# Mixed Review and Test Prep

**5** What's 32 added to 15?

**A.** 79          **B.** 69          **C.** 67          **D.** 47

**From Paces to Feet**

# Which Unit?

Circle **centimeter** or **meter** to show which unit you would use to measure the object. (HINT: Smaller things can be measured better with centimeters.)

**Family Connection**

Students are learning to measure in centimeters and in meters. You might want to talk with your child about these units of measurement. You can point to objects around your home and ask your child whether each object should be measured using centimeters or meters.

**1**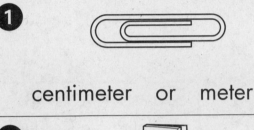

centimeter or meter

**2**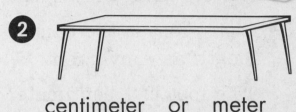

centimeter or meter

**3**

centimeter or meter

**4**

centimeter or meter

**5**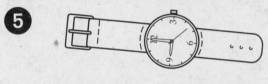

centimeter or meter

**6**

centimeter or meter

**7**

centimeter or meter

**8**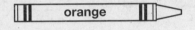

centimeter or meter

# Mixed Review and Test Prep

**9** You have 2 quarters, 3 dimes, and 1 nickel. How much more money do you need to have $1?

**A.** 5¢          **B.** 15¢          **C.** 25¢          **D.** 85¢

**From Paces to Feet**

# Whose Foot?

**1** Whose foot is it? Read all clues. Write the person's name by the measurement.

- Pepe's foot is 2 centimeters shorter than Amy's foot.

- Rick's foot is the same length as Amy's foot.

- TJ's foot is 1 centimeter longer than Pepe's foot.

- Rosario's foot is longer than Amy's foot, but shorter than Ben's foot.

- Max's foot is the smallest of all!

17 centimeters: _____

18 centimeters: _____

19 centimeters: _____

20 centimeters: _____

20 centimeters: _____

21 centimeters: _____

22 centimeters: _____

**Family Connection**

Students continue to learn about metric measurement by using centimeter rulers and metersticks (or the centimeter squares and 100-centimeter-long "meter strips" they made in school) to measure objects and parts of their bodies. You can help your child by providing extra practice in measuring things around the your home.

**Interesting Tidbit**

Most third graders' feet measure around 20 centimeters in length.

# Mixed Review and Test Prep

**2** What is 3 hours after 9:00 A.M.?

**A.** 12:00 P.M.  **B.** 1:30 P.M.  **C.** 11:00 A.M.  **D.** 10:30 A.M.

**From Paces to Feet**

# Reach for the Sky!

The students in Mr. Borke's class used centimeters to measure how high they could reach without standing on their tiptoes. Here's their data:

**Family Connection**

Students continue to gather data by measuring objects and distances. And as they organize and analyze a data set, they look for what is typical, as well as for the range and other features of the data. Ask your child to explain how he or she made the line plot on this page.

| Mark | 148 | Yoshi | 150 | Chi Wan | 156 | Jacob | 155 |
|------|-----|-------|-----|---------|-----|-------|-----|
| Tara | 150 | Ebony | 153 | Samir | 152 | Maria | 154 |
| Imani | 155 | Morgan | 152 | Camille | 150 | Alyssa | 157 |
| Nadir | 154 | Kira | 156 | Evan | 154 | Tory | 153 |

**1** Use the data to make a line plot. Write the numbers in order. Mark an **X** above the line for each measurement.

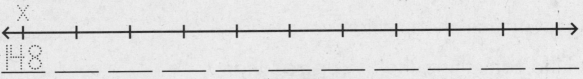

**centimeters**

**2** The students' reaches ranged from _____ to _____ centimeters.

**3** What was the typical reach for this class? _____

## Mixed Review and Test Prep

**4** You have 86 buttons in two boxes.
One box has 39 buttons in it.
How many buttons are in the other box?

**A.** 125          **B.** 57          **C.** 47          **D.** 40

# More Comparisons

Use a meterstick or the paper "meter strip" you made in school.

**Family Connection**

Students continue to investigate linear measurement and to compare the lengths of objects. They are becoming proficient in using a meterstick and in measuring with centimeters. If your child does not have a tool for measuring in centimeters, he or she may use an inch ruler, yard stick, or tape measure.

**1** Find something that is **taller** than you are. How tall is it? _____

**2** How much taller than you is it? _____

**3** Find something that is **wider** than your shoulders. How wide is it? _____

**4** How much wider than your shoulders is it? _____

**5** Find something that is **shorter** than your foot. How long is it? _____

**6** How much shorter than your foot is it? _____

**7** Find something that is **longer** than your pencil. How long is it? _____

**8** How much longer than your pencil is it? _____

## Mixed Review and Test Prep

**9** You saved 75¢. Which 3 coupons did you use?

A. | Save 50¢ | Save 25¢ | Save 10¢ |

C. | Save 35¢ | Save 25¢ | Save 15¢ |

B. | Save 45¢ | Save 25¢ | Save 15¢ |

D. | Save 25¢ | Save 25¢ | Save 10¢ |

**From Paces to Feet**

# A Chair for Baby Bear

After Goldilocks broke Baby Bear's chair, his parents decided to build a brand-new one.

First, they measured the seat height of his old chair: 26 centimeters.

Then, they measured Baby Bear's leg length (from his knee to the floor): 29 centimeters.

Well, what do you know! Baby Bear really did need a new chair!

**1** Baby Bear's legs had grown at least

_____ centimeters.

**2** If the back of his new chair measures the same as the seat height, how tall will his new chair be? _____

**3** If Mama Bear's chair is twice as tall as Baby Bear's, how tall is it? _____

**4** If Papa Bear's chair is twice as tall as Mama Bear's, how tall is it? _____

## Mixed Review and Test Prep

**5** How far is it from 45 to 100?

**A.** 35        **B.** 45        **C.** 55        **D.** 65

# Just Right!

**1** Draw the three bears sitting on their chairs.

REMEMBER: Mama's chair is twice as tall as Baby's chair. And Papa's chair is twice as tall as Mama's chair.

**Family Connection**

Students continue to work on determining what size furniture fits them best. They have been measuring and comparing their body sizes to the sizes of the furniture in the classroom. You might want to ask your child to explain his or her thinking about the relative sizes of the drawings required on this page.

**Baby Bear**          **Mama Bear**          **Papa Bear**

## Mixed Review and Test Prep

**2** Which shape pattern below matches **clap, stomp, tap**?

A. △ ○ □    B. △ ○ ○    C. ○ □ □    D. △ △ □

# The Balobbyland Pool

Here are plans for a pool in Balobbyland:

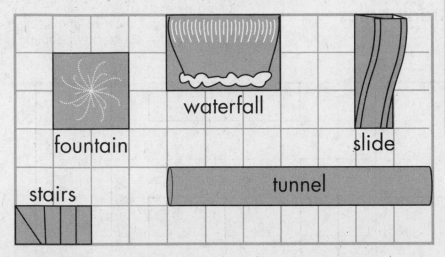

**Family Connection**

Students have been designing spaces for Balobbies, which are mythical, tiny people just a few centimeters tall. This activity has been helping your child develop an awareness of centimeters and how to use them to measure objects and short distances.

**1** What are the dimensions of the pool?
_____ × _____ centimeters

**2** What are the dimensions of the slide?
_____ × _____ centimeters

**3** What are the dimensions of the tunnel?
_____ × _____ centimeters

**4** What are the dimensions of the fountain?
_____ × _____ centimeters

## Mixed Review and Test Prep

**5** 10 students were surveyed to find out what their favorite color was. Their favorite color was **not** red. Which graph shows the data?

**A.**

| red | ✓✓✓✓✓ |
|-----|-------|
| blue | ✓✓ |
| green | ✓✓✓ |

**B.**

| red | ✓✓✓✓ |
|-----|------|
| blue | ✓✓✓ |
| green | ✓✓✓ |

**C.**

| red | ✓✓✓✓✓ |
|-----|-------|
| blue | ✓✓✓✓ |
| green | ✓ |

**D.**

| red | ✓✓✓✓ |
|-----|------|
| blue | ✓✓✓✓✓ |
| green | ✓ |

# The Balobbyland Library

Here are plans for the library in Balobbyland. The rectangles are bookshelves.

**Family Connection**

Students have been designing spaces for Balobbies, mythical, tiny people who are only a few centimeters tall. This page shows a "bird's-eye" view of plans for a library for these tiny people.

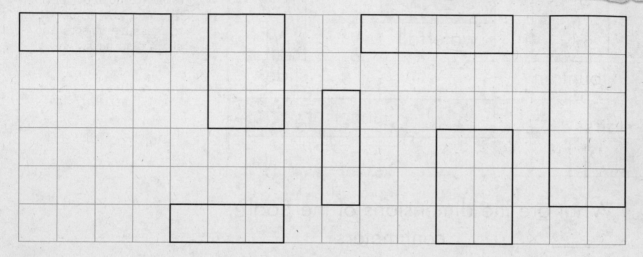

**1** Color the shelves that are 1 × 4 centimeters red.

**2** Color the shelves that are 2 × 5 centimeters blue.

**3** Color the shelves that are 3 × 1 centimeters yellow.

**4** Color the shelves that are 2 × 3 centimeters green.

**5** Draw a table that measures 3 × 3 centimeters.

# Mixed Review and Test Prep

**6** What is the secret number?

If you count by 10's, you say this number.
This number doubled is between 40 and 70.

**A.** 40          **B.** 35          **C.** 30          **D.** 25

**From Paces to Feet**

# In the Neighborhood

Think about the Balobbyland neighborhood you made at school.

**Family Connection**

Students have been designing neighborhoods for Balobbies, the tiny "people" the class has been working with to develop students' understanding of measuring with centimeters. **Questions you might ask your child:** "What spaces did you design for your Balobbyland neighborhood? What things did you put in those spaces? How big did you make them?"

**1** What different spaces did you design for your Balobbyland neighborhood?

_____

_____

**2** Which space was your favorite? Why?

_____

_____

**3** Which space was the largest? _____

**4** Which space was the smallest? _____

**5** If you were to design another space for your Balobbyland neighborhood, what would it be like?

_____

_____

# Mixed Review and Test Prep

**6** There are 46 legs in Room 222, including the teacher's legs. How many students are in this class?

**A.** 20      **B.** 22      **C.** 23      **D.** 25

Name _____                                    Date _____

# Sweet Sixteen

Find 16 pennies (or other counters).

**Family Connection**

Students have been arranging objects in groups of 2, 4, 5, and so on, and then skip counting to find the total amount. If your child is working on this page at home, he or she will need to use pennies, beans, or other small objects as counters.

**1** Arrange your counters in groups of 2. Draw the groups.

How many groups did you make?          _____
Count your groups by 2's. Write the numbers.

2, 4, _____

**2** Arrange your counters in groups of 4. Draw the groups.

How many groups did you make?          _____
Count your groups by 4's. Write the numbers.

_____

**3** Make a different number of equal groups.

How many groups did you make?          _____

How many counters are in each group?          _____
Skip count to find the total. Write the numbers.

_____

## Mixed Review and Test Prep

**4** How many faces does this figure have?

**A.** 12          **B.** 8          **C.** 6          **D.** 4

Name _____                    Date _____

# Skip Your Way to 100!

Fill in the missing numbers.
(Look for patterns!)

**Family Connection**

Students have been using the 100 chart to explore number patterns and to skip count. Ask your child to show you how to use the chart to skip count by 3's to 30.

**1** 2, 4, 6, _____, _____, _____

**2** 3, 6, 9, _____, _____, _____

**3** 4, 8, 12, _____, _____, _____

**4** 5, 10, 15, _____, _____, _____

**5** 6, 12, 18, _____, _____, _____

**6** 7, 14, 21, _____, _____, _____

**7** 8, 16, 24, _____, _____, _____

**8** 10, 20, 30, _____, _____, _____

| 1 | 2 | 3 | 4 | 5 | 6 | 7 | 8 | 9 | 10 |
|---|---|---|---|---|---|---|---|---|---|
| 11 | 12 | 13 | 14 | 15 | 16 | 17 | 18 | 19 | 20 |
| 21 | 22 | 23 | 24 | 25 | 26 | 27 | 28 | 29 | 30 |
| 31 | 32 | 33 | 34 | 35 | 36 | 37 | 38 | 39 | 40 |
| 41 | 42 | 43 | 44 | 45 | 46 | 47 | 48 | 49 | 50 |
| 51 | 52 | 53 | 54 | 55 | 56 | 57 | 58 | 59 | 60 |
| 61 | 62 | 63 | 64 | 65 | 66 | 67 | 68 | 69 | 70 |
| 71 | 72 | 73 | 74 | 75 | 76 | 77 | 78 | 79 | 80 |
| 81 | 82 | 83 | 84 | 85 | 86 | 87 | 88 | 89 | 90 |
| 91 | 92 | 93 | 94 | 95 | 96 | 97 | 98 | 99 | 100 |

# Mixed Review and Test Prep

**9** You have these two blocks.
Which shape below can you fill?

A.

C.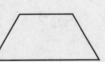

B.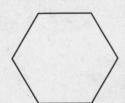

D.

**Landmarks in the Hundreds**

# Is That a Factor?

Circle **all** the factors for the number given. Then choose **one** of the factors and write the numbers that complete the sentences for that factor.

**Family Connection**

Students are becoming familiar with factors (numbers you can count by to reach a given number). For example, 2 is a factor of 10 (2, 4, 6, 8, 10). Name a number such as 8 or 12 and ask your child to find the factors of that number (Factors of 8: 1, 2, 4, 8; factors of 12: 1, 2, 3, 4, 6, 12)

**1** Find the factors of 18.

| ① | ② | ③ | 4 | 5 | ⑥ | 7 | 8 | ⑨ | 10 |
|---|---|---|---|---|---|---|---|---|----|
| 11 | 12 | 13 | 14 | 15 | 16 | 17 | 18 | | |

_3_ is a factor of 18.

How many _3_ 's in 18? _6_

____ × ____ = 18

**2** Find the factors of 20.

| 1 | 2 | 3 | 4 | 5 | 6 | 7 | 8 | 9 | 10 |
|---|---|---|---|---|---|---|---|---|----|
| 11 | 12 | 13 | 14 | 15 | 16 | 17 | 18 | 19 | 20 |

____ is a factor of 20.

How many ____ 's in 20? ____

____ × ____ = 20

**3** Find the factors of 24.

| 1 | 2 | 3 | 4 | 5 | 6 | 7 | 8 | 9 | 10 |
|---|---|---|---|---|---|---|---|---|----|
| 11 | 12 | 13 | 14 | 15 | 16 | 17 | 18 | 19 | 20 |
| 21 | 22 | 23 | 24 | | | | | | |

____ is a factor of 24.

How many ____ 's in 24? ____

____ × ____ = 24

# Mixed Review and Test Prep

**4** Which shows 25¢?

A.

C.

B.

D.

**Landmarks in the Hundreds**

# Will You Land on 100?

Some of these numbers are factors of 100 and some of them aren't:

**3   4   10   12   15   20**

**Family Connection**

Students have been using the 100 chart to find factors of 100 (numbers you can count by to reach 100). Ask your child to show you how he or she can tell whether or not a given number is a factor of 100. Also ask your child how many "jumps" of each factor it takes to land exactly on 100.

Which ones are?
Which ones aren't?

You can use the 100 chart to help you find all the factors of 100.

Not to worry!

Just count by the number.

If you land on 100, then you know that the number you are counting by is a factor of 100.

| 1 | 2 | 3 | 4 | 5 | 6 | 7 | 8 | 9 | 10 |
|---|---|---|---|---|---|---|---|---|---|
| 11 | 12 | 13 | 14 | 15 | 16 | 17 | 18 | 19 | 20 |
| 21 | 22 | 23 | 24 | 25 | 26 | 27 | 28 | 29 | 30 |
| 31 | 32 | 33 | 34 | 35 | 36 | 37 | 38 | 39 | 40 |
| 41 | 42 | 43 | 44 | 45 | 46 | 47 | 48 | 49 | 50 |
| 51 | 52 | 53 | 54 | 55 | 56 | 57 | 58 | 59 | 60 |
| 61 | 62 | 63 | 64 | 65 | 66 | 67 | 68 | 69 | 70 |
| 71 | 72 | 73 | 74 | 75 | 76 | 77 | 78 | 79 | 80 |
| 81 | 82 | 83 | 84 | 85 | 86 | 87 | 88 | 89 | 90 |
| 91 | 92 | 93 | 94 | 95 | 96 | 97 | 98 | 99 | 100 |

**1** These numbers **are** factors of 100: _____

**2** These numbers are **not** factors of 100: _____

**3** Can you find other factors of 100? Write them below.

_____

# Mixed Review and Test Prep

**4** Which number combination is **not** a way to show 10?

**A.** 5 + 5

**C.** 4 + 3 + 4

**B.** 1 + 8 + 1

**D.** 2 + 2 + 6

# 100 Stamps!

Each picture below shows a block of stamps. Tell how many of each block are needed to make 100 stamps.

**1** _____ blocks of 10 stamps each make 100 stamps.

**2** _____ blocks of 5 stamps each make 100 stamps.

**3** _____ blocks of _____ stamps each make 100 stamps.

**4** _____ blocks of _____ stamps each make 100 stamps.

**5** _____ blocks of _____ stamps each make 100 stamps.

# Mixed Review and Test Prep

**6** Which number completes the sentence?

$4 + 4 +$ _____ $= 11$

**A.** 3          **B.** 4          **C.** 5          **D.** 7

## Landmarks in the Hundreds

# Follow the Factor Road

**1** Look at each multiplication expression below. Does it equal 100? If it does, color the box.

| 10 × 10 | | | |
| 6 × 15 | 5 × 20 | 15 × 2 | 3 × 30 |
| 30 × 4 | 4 × 25 | 2 × 40 | |
| | 100 × 1 | 10 × 8 | |
| 25 × 8 | 2 × 50 | | 20 × 5 |
| | 4 × 12 | 3 × 40 | |
| 20 × 6 | 8 × 15 | 50 × 2 | 5 × 25 |

25 × 4    40 × 5

Beach    Café    Amusement Park    MALL

**2** Where does the "Factors of 100 Road" lead?

_____

# Mixed Review and Test Prep

**3** If one pack of juice contains 6 boxes, how many boxes are in 2 packs?

**A.** 12          **B.** 10          **C.** 8          **D.** 4

# Coin Count

Tell how many coins it takes to make one dollar.

1. _____  make one dollar.

2. _____  make one dollar.

3. _____  make one dollar.

4. _____ make one dollar.

**Interesting Tidbit**

In the 1700s, Americans used silver coins that were called "Pieces of Eight." Each of these coins was equal to about one dollar, and could be broken into 8 "pieces," or bits. About how much would one "piece" be worth in cents?

5. Create a new coin. Give the coin a value.

- The value cannot be 1¢, 5¢, 10¢, 25¢, 50¢, or $1.

- You must be able to make $1 using **only** your coins.

My coin is called _____.

My coin is worth _____ ¢.

_____ of my coins make $1.

**Draw the coin here.**

# Mixed Review and Test Prep

6. Which coins total 15¢?

A.   B.   C.   D.

**Landmarks in the Hundreds**

# Multiples of 100

**1** How many ...

- 5's in 100? _____

- 5's in 200? _____

- 5's in 300? _____

Look at the number of 5's in 100, 200, and 300. Do you see a pattern? Explain.

_____

_____

**Family Connection**

Students build on previous work with factors of 100, such as 5 and 25, and use these factors when working with multiples of 100, such as 200 and 300. **Questions you might ask your child:** "How could you find the number of 5's in 400? How could you find the number of 25's? Are these two questions related? ... How?"

**2** How many ...

- 25's in 100? _____

- 25's in 200? _____

- 25's in 300? _____

Look at the number of 25's in 100, 200, and 300. Do you see a pattern? Explain.

_____

_____

# Mixed Review and Test Prep

**3** There are 18 children. How many seats will be empty?

**A.** 2      **B.** 3      **C.** 4      **D.** 6

# Money Match

Draw a line between each group of coins and its value.

**Family Connection**

Students have been investigating the numbers of nickels, dimes, and quarters in monetary amounts ranging from $1 to $5. Ask your child to explain how he or she would find the number of quarters in $4.25.

 8                     $2.50

**2** 35                     $4.00

**3** 25                     $2.90

**1** 16                     $3.50

**1** 29                     $2.00

**6** 50                     $1.25

# Mixed Review and Test Prep

Jeb used pattern blocks like this to cover the larger shape to the right. How many blocks did he use?

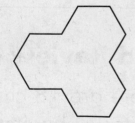

**A.** 9          **B.** 6          **C.** 4          **D.** 3

**Landmarks in the Hundreds**

# How Many 25's?

Complete the chart. Then use the chart to answer the questions.

**Family Connection**
Students have been developing strategies for solving multiplication and division problems by using their knowledge of factors and multiples. For example, students find how many 25's are in 100, and then use this information to find how many 25's are in other, related numbers, such as 275 and 350. Ask your child to explain how he or she finds the number of 25's in 450.

**1**

| Number | How many 25's? |
|--------|----------------|
| 100    |                |
| 200    |                |
| 300    |                |
| 400    |                |
| 500    |                |

**2** How many 25's are in 275? _____
Explain how you know.

_____

_____

**3** How many 25's are in 450? _____
Explain how you know.

_____

_____

# Mixed Review and Test Prep

**4** There were 24 birds in a tree. Then a dog barked and scared 8 of them away. How many birds were left in the tree?

**A.** 12        **B.** 16        **C.** 28        **D.** 32

**Landmarks in the Hundreds**

# A Day at the Beach

Solve each problem. Use coins or drawings if you wish.

**Family Connection**

Students continue to develop their understanding of using factors to solve multiplication and division problems involving money. Ask your child to show you what he or she did to solve Exercises 1 and 2 on this page.

**1** If Rob buys 4 ice cream cones, how much will he spend? _____

**2** The Surf Shop rents rafts for $2.50. How much will 3 friends pay to rent one raft each? _____

$1.75

**3** The beach charges 50 cents for each person. Ana has $6.00. How many people can Ana bring to the beach? Explain your answer.

_____

_____

_____

**Interesting Tidbit**

The ice cream cone became popular at the St. Louis World's Fair in 1904. An ice cream seller ran out of dishes and began putting ice cream in pastry cones. It was a success!

# Mixed Review and Test Prep

**4** Lightbulbs come in packs of 2. How many bulbs are in 8 packs?

2

A. 16          C. 10

B. 14          D. 6

**Landmarks in the Hundreds**

# Division Puzzle

Shade the division problem that best matches the situation.

**Family Connection**
Students are learning how to write and solve division problems, for example, 27 ÷ 3 (also recorded as 3)27). Describe a division situation, such as 12 crackers being shared equally among 3 children. Ask your child to write this problem using a division symbol, and then to find the solution.

**1** 15 seats are put in rows of 5.

**2** 21 children are placed in groups of 3.

**3** 40 books are put in rows of 8.

**4** 6 friends share 30 stickers.

**5** 64 counters are placed in 8 rows.

**6** 48 oranges are put in 6 bags.

**7** 45 grapes are shared among 5 friends.

**8** 4 children share 32 peanuts.

**9** 54 players are on 9 teams.

**10** 14 plants are planted in 7 pots.

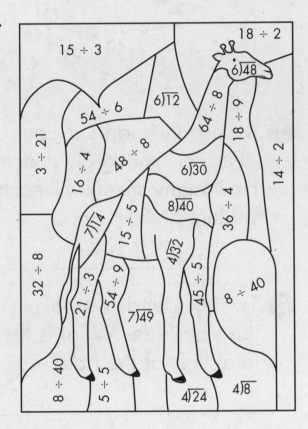

# Mixed Review and Test Prep

**11** You have 24 pennies. How many more pennies do you need to make $1.00?

**A.** 26          **B.** 51          **C.** 66          **D.** 76

# Multiplying and Dividing

Use the information in the pictures. Write a multiplication or division sentence to solve each problem.

**Family Connection**

Students have been working on multiplication and division problems, and using symbols to record their work. Ask your child to describe why he or she chose multiplication or division to solve one of the problems on this page.

**1** Mr. Grant shares a pack of paper among 30 students. How many sheets will each student get?

_____

**2** Mindy has $1.25 to spend. How many pencils can she buy?

_____

**3** Twenty friends are taking the train ride. What is the total cost of the ride?

_____

**4** If Dan buys 4 packs of paper, how many sheets will he have?

_____

# Mixed Review and Test Prep

**5** How many pencils does Tanya have in all?

**Tanya's Pencil Inventory**
Black pencils
Red pencils
Blue pencils

**A.** 18          **B.** 15          **C.** 7          **D.** 4

**Landmarks in the Hundreds**

# Count to 1000

Complete the charts.
Then use them to answer
the questions.

**Family Connection**

Students are building on previous work with factors of 100 as they look for patterns in numbers to 1000. Ask your child to tell you how many 20's are in 600, and then to explain how he or she found the answer.

**1**

| Number | How many 20's? |
|--------|----------------|
| 100    | 5              |
| 200    |                |
| 300    |                |
| 400    |                |
| 500    |                |

**2**

| Number | How many 50's? |
|--------|----------------|
| 100    | 2              |
| 200    |                |
| 300    |                |
| 400    |                |
| 500    |                |

**3** How many 20's are in 1000? _____
How did you find your answer?

_____

**4** How many 50's are in 1000? _____
How did you find your answer?

_____

**5** How could you use the number of 50's in
1000 to find the number of 25's in 1000?

_____

_____

# Mixed Review and Test Prep

**6** Which group of coins is **not** worth 50¢?

**A.** 2 quarters    **B.** 20 nickels    **C.** 5 dimes    **D.** 50 pennies

# On the Chart

Here is part of Neil's 1000 chart.
Use it and the puzzle key below
to help you solve these problems:

**1** How many pages
are in Neil's
science book?          _____

**2** How many cards
are in 8 decks?          _____

**3** How many
students are in
Neil's school?          _____

**4** How many napkins
are in 4 packs?          _____

**5** Find something in school
or at home that matches
another number on the chart.

_____

| 321 | 322 | 323 | 324 | 325 | 326 | 327 | 328 | 329 | 330 |
| 331 | 332 | 333 | 334 | 335 | 336 | 337 | 338 |     | 340 |
| 341 | 342 | 343 | 344 | 345 | 346 | 347 | 348 | 349 | 350 |
| 351 | 352 | 353 | 354 | 355 | 356 | 357 | 358 | 359 | 360 |
| 361 | 362 | 363 | 364 | 365 | 366 | 367 | 368 | 369 | 370 |
| 371 | 372 | 373 | 374 | 375 | 376 | 377 |     | 379 | 380 |
| 381 | 382 | 383 | 384 | 385 | 386 | 387 | 388 | 389 | 390 |
| 391 | 392 | 393 | 394 | 395 | 396 | 397 | 398 | 399 |     |
| 401 | 402 | 403 | 404 | 405 | 406 | 407 | 408 | 409 | 410 |
| 411 | 412 | 413 | 414 | 415 |     | 417 | 418 | 419 | 420 |
| 421 | 422 | 423 | 424 | 425 | 426 | 427 | 428 | 429 | 430 |
| 431 | 432 | 433 | 434 | 435 | 436 | 437 | 438 | 439 | 440 |
| 441 | 442 | 443 | 444 | 445 | 446 | 447 | 448 | 449 | 450 |

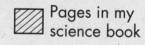 Napkins in 4 packs          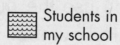 Pages in my science book

Students in my school          Playing cards in 8 decks

# Mixed Review and Test Prep

**6** Which of the following does **not** equal 20?

**A.** 20 − 20          **C.** 24 − 4

**B.** 33 − 13          **D.** 20 − 0

**Landmarks in the Hundreds**

# How Far Is It?

Here is part of a 1000 chart. Use it to help you answer these questions:

**Family Connection**

Students have been counting on a 1000 chart and using multiples of 1000 (such as 20, 25, and 50) to find the distance between a given pair of numbers. Choose one of the problems on this page and have your child explain his or her answer.

## How far is it from ...

**1** 500 to 580?  _____

**2** 525 to 575?  _____

**3** 450 to 600?  _____

**4** 475 to 575?  _____

**5** 440 to 560?  _____

**6** 450 to 625?  _____

**7** 470 to 510?  _____

**8** 480 to 620?  _____

**9** 450 to 575?  _____

| 451 | 452 | 453 | 454 | 455 | 456 | 457 | 458 | 459 | 460 |
| 461 | 462 | 463 | 464 | 465 | 466 | 467 | 468 | 469 | 470 |
| 471 | 472 | 473 | 474 | 475 | 476 | 477 | 478 | 479 | 480 |
| 481 | 482 | 483 | 484 | 485 | 486 | 487 | 488 | 489 | 490 |
| 491 | 492 | 493 | 494 | 495 | 496 | 497 | 498 | 499 | 500 |
| 501 | 502 | 503 | 504 | 505 | 506 | 507 | 508 | 509 | 510 |
| 511 | 512 | 513 | 514 | 515 | 516 | 517 | 518 | 519 | 520 |
| 521 | 522 | 523 | 524 | 525 | 526 | 527 | 528 | 529 | 530 |
| 531 | 532 | 533 | 534 | 535 | 536 | 537 | 538 | 539 | 540 |
| 541 | 542 | 543 | 544 | 545 | 546 | 547 | 548 | 549 | 550 |
| 551 | 552 | 553 | 554 | 555 | 556 | 557 | 558 | 559 | 560 |
| 561 | 562 | 563 | 564 | 565 | 566 | 567 | 568 | 569 | 570 |
| 571 | 572 | 573 | 574 | 575 | 576 | 577 | 578 | 579 | 580 |
| 581 | 582 | 583 | 584 | 585 | 586 | 587 | 588 | 589 | 590 |
| 591 | 592 | 593 | 594 | 595 | 596 | 597 | 598 | 599 | 600 |
| 601 | 602 | 603 | 604 | 605 | 606 | 607 | 608 | 609 | 610 |
| 611 | 612 | 613 | 614 | 615 | 616 | 617 | 618 | 619 | 620 |
| 621 | 622 | 623 | 624 | 625 | 626 | 627 | 628 | 629 | 630 |

# Mixed Review and Test Prep

**10** How many cubes does it take to make this shape?

**A.** 8          **B.** 10          **C.** 12          **D.** 14

# Going Up!

Write the net change for each elevator trip. Use the picture to help you.

**Family Connection**

Students have been using a picture of the floors in a sky-scraper to learn how to move up and down a number line to show positive and negative changes. Ask your child to show you how to find the **net change**, while moving up and down the floors in the skyscraper.

| Starting Floor | Ending Floor | Net Change |
|---|---|---|
| B2 | 1 | +3 |
| 2 | B3 | −5 |
| 4 | 6 | |
| 0 | B4 | |
| B2 | 5 | |
| B3 | 3 | |
| 6 | B2 | |
| B1 | B5 | |
| 0 | 5 | |

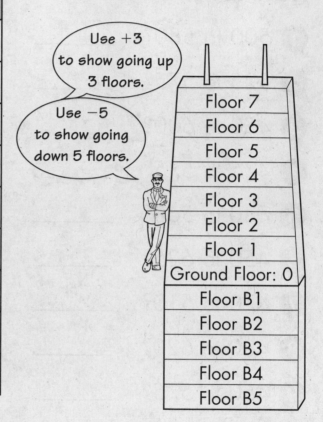

Use +3 to show going up 3 floors.

Use −5 to show going down 5 floors.

Floor 7
Floor 6
Floor 5
Floor 4
Floor 3
Floor 2
Floor 1
Ground Floor: 0
Floor B1
Floor B2
Floor B3
Floor B4
Floor B5

# Mixed Review and Test Prep

**10** Which is **not** a way to show 5?

**A.** 7 − 2          **C.** 2 + 0 + 3

**B.** 3 + 1 + 1          **D.** 8 − 4

# Comparing Elevator Trips

Write the net change for each trip.
Use the picture to help you.

**Family Connection**

Students have been comparing the net changes for different elevator trips. Ask your child to create two elevator trips that have the same net change. Talk about net change if you and your child take an elevator trip together.

| | Starting Floor | Ending Floor | Net Change |
|---|---|---|---|
| **1** | B2 | 4 | |
| **2** | B2 | B4 | |
| **3** | 4 | B2 | |
| **4** | 4 | 2 | |
| **5** | B4 | B2 | |
| **6** | B4 | 2 | |

Floor 4
Floor 3
Floor 2
Floor 1
Ground Floor: 0
Floor B1
Floor B2
Floor B3
Floor B4
Floor B5

**Interesting Tidbit**

The Sears Tower in Chicago, the tallest skyscraper in the United States, is 1454 feet tall.

**7** Name two problems above that result in the same net change. Why do they have the same net change?

_____

_____

**8** Make up a trip that has the same net change as the trips you listed in Problem 7.

_____

## Mixed Review and Test Prep

**9** How many bikes can be made with 20 wheels?

**A.** 40      **B.** 20      **C.** 10      **D.** 5

# Special Elevator Buttons

Use these special elevator buttons. They show how many floors you want to change and in which direction.

**Family Connection**

In class, students have explored finding the net change produced by a series of three or more individual changes such as −3, −1, and +2. They have also found different ways of making the same net change. Ask your child to explain his or her answers in Exercises 3 and 4.

**1** Start on Floor 3.
Press −2 −3 +1.

End on Floor _____.

Net change: _____

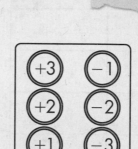

Floor 7
Floor 6
Floor 5
Floor 4
Floor 3
Floor 2
Floor 1
Ground Floor: 0
Floor B1
Floor B2
Floor B3
Floor B4
Floor B5

**2** Start on Floor 3.
Press +2 −3 −3.

End on Floor _____.

Net change: _____

Write three ways to make each net change.
Use at least three buttons for each way.

**3** Net change: +1

_____

_____

_____

**4** Net change: −3

_____

_____

_____

# Mixed Review and Test Prep

**5** Which sum is closest to 20?

**A.** 7 + 3 + 7   **B.** 8 + 2 + 9   **C.** 5 + 5 + 8   **D.** 7 + 7 + 9

### Up and Down the Number Line

## It's in the Cards

Fill in the blank change cards
to make the net change shown.
You can use these change cards:

| -3 | -2 | -1 | 0 | +1 | +2 | +3 |

**1** Net change: −2

| +3 | -2 | +1 | -3 | 0 | | |

| | |
|---|---|
| Floor 7 | |
| Floor 6 | |
| Floor 5 | |
| Floor 4 | |
| Floor 3 | |
| Floor 2 | |
| Floor 1 | |
| Ground Floor: 0 | |
| Floor B1 | |
| Floor B2 | |
| Floor B3 | |
| Floor B4 | |
| Floor B5 | |

**2** Net change: +3

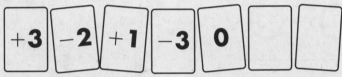

| -3 | -1 | +2 | -1 | +2 | | |

**3** Net change: −5

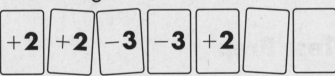

| +2 | +2 | -3 | -3 | +2 | | |

**4** Net change: 0

| +1 | +3 | -2 | 0 | +1 | | |

## Mixed Review and Test Prep

**5** What is the value of these coins?

**A.** 13¢ **B.** 25¢ **C.** 35¢ **D.** 85¢

# Up and Down

Pete got on an elevator on the ground floor. He went up and down by pressing these twenty change buttons:

$(+3) \rightarrow (-2) \rightarrow (+2) \rightarrow (-1) \rightarrow (-3)$

$(+3) \rightarrow (+1) \rightarrow (-3) \rightarrow (0) \rightarrow (+3)$

$(+2) \rightarrow (-2) \rightarrow (-2) \rightarrow (+3) \rightarrow (-3)$

$(+1) \rightarrow (-3) \rightarrow (+2) \rightarrow (-2) \rightarrow (-1)$

**1** On what floor did his elevator trip end? _____

# Mixed Review and Test Prep

**2** How many students were surveyed?

A. 44        C. 23

B. 24        D. 19

**Are you wearing stripes?**

| Yes | No |
|-----|-----|
| ||||  ||||  |  ||||  |||| |

**3** How many more students were wearing stripes than were not?

A. 5          B. 9          C. 14          D. 23

**Up and Down the Number Line**

# Missing Starts and Changes

Oops! The numbers have worn off some of the change buttons. Write the missing numbers on the buttons.

**Family Connection**

Students solve problems where either the starting floor or net change number is missing. Ask your child to choose one of the exercises on this page and explain how he or she found the missing number.

| | Starting Floor | Changes | | Ending Floor |
|---|---|---|---|---|
| **1** | 3 | (−2) | ( ) | B2 |
| **2** | 4 | ( ) | (+3) | 6 |
| **3** | B4 | (+3) | ( ) | B3 |
| **4** | 0 | ( ) | (+3) | 1 |

Forgetful Fran took some elevator rides and can't remember her starting floor. Write the missing starting floor for Fran's trips.

| | Starting Floor | Changes | | Ending Floor |
|---|---|---|---|---|
| **5** | | (−3) | (−1) | 2 |
| **6** | | (−2) | (+3) | 1 |
| **7** | | (+3) | (−1) | B1 |

# Mixed Review and Test Prep

**8** Which does **not** make 10?

**A.** $4 + 6$    **B.** $7 + 3$    **C.** $2 + 9$    **D.** $5 + 5$

## Up and Down the Number Line

# Mystery Trips

Use these change buttons to
solve the problems:

**Family Connection**

Ask your child to make up an
elevator problem like the ones on
this page. Have your child explain
how to solve the problem.

I started on Floor 1
and pressed three change buttons
to arrive at Floor B3. What buttons
might I have pressed?

I started on Floor 5 and
pressed two change buttons to
arrive at Floor 3. What buttons
might I have pressed?

**1** _____

**2** _____

I got on the elevator
and pressed +3 +2 +2 to arrive
at Floor 3. On what floor did
I start?

I got on the elevator and
pressed +1 0 −3 to arrive at the
Ground Floor. On what floor
did I start?

**3** _____

**4** _____

I started on Floor 4
and pressed six change buttons to
arrive at Floor B1. What buttons
might I have pressed?

**5** _____

# Mixed Review and Test Prep

**6** Find the number that comes next: 97, 98, 99, 100, ____

**A.** 101      **B.** 200      **C.** 1001      **D.** 110

**Up and Down the Number Line**

# What Floor Do You Want?

For each problem, make up an elevator trip that has 4 changes. Use these change buttons.

$(-3)$ $(-2)$ $(-1)$ $(0)$ $(+1)$ $(+2)$ $(+3)$

**Family Connection**

In class, students played a game in which they arranged a set of change cards to make the elevator stop on as many different floors as possible. **Questions you might ask your child:** "How can you avoid returning to the same floor?" "What happens if you use 0 for one of the change buttons?"

In the chart write the floor you start on, each of your changes, and the floor you move to.

**1** 

| Starting Floor: _____ ||
| --- | --- |
| **Change** | **New Location** |
|  |  |
|  |  |
|  |  |
|  |  |

**2** 

| Starting Floor: _____ ||
| --- | --- |
| **Change** | **New Location** |
|  |  |
|  |  |
|  |  |
|  |  |

If you count the starting floor, how many different floors did you visit ...

**3** in Problem 1? _____    **4** in Problem 2? _____

**5** What do you think is the **greatest** number of different floors you can visit with 4 change buttons if you count the starting floor? _____

## Mixed Review and Test Prep

**6** How many toes are on 6 feet?

**A.** 25          **B.** 30          **C.** 50          **D.** 60

# Elevator Graphs

For each elevator trip, show
a way to graph the trip on
the elevator diagram.

**1) Start: B2
Changes:**

+3
−2
−3

| 5 |
| 4 |
| 3 |
| 2 |
| 1 |
| 0 |
| B1 |
| B2 |
| B3 |
| B4 |

**2 Start: 0
Changes:**

−1
+2
+3
−3

| 5 |
| 4 |
| 3 |
| 2 |
| 1 |
| 0 |
| B1 |
| B2 |
| B3 |
| B4 |

**3) Explain how to read the graph you drew in
Problem 1.**

_____

_____

**4 Draw or explain how you would show a change of 0.
(Use another sheet of paper if you need to.)**

# Mixed Review and Test Prep

**5 How many more students chose
bananas than oranges?**

**A.** 6  **C.** 3

**B.** 4  **D.** 2

| What's your favorite fruit? | |
|---|---|
| Oranges | 🚶🚶🚶🚶 |
| Bananas | 🚶🚶🚶🚶🚶🚶 |
| Apples | 🚶🚶🚶 |

**Up and Down the Number Line**

# The Graph Says It All

The graph shows an elevator trip.
Each dot shows a stop during the trip.

**Family Connection**
Students are interpreting graphs that represent elevator trips. Ask your child to explain how he or she continued the pattern on the graph.

**1** The first point on the left side of the graph shows the starting floor. Which floor is it?

_____

**2** Which 3 changes does the graph show?

_____  _____  _____

**3** On what floor is the elevator now?

_____

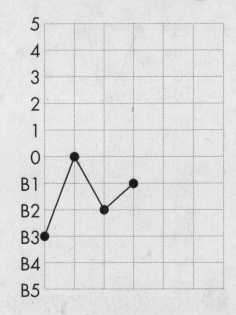

**4** Starting at the floor in Problem 3, show on the graph another set of the same changes you wrote in Problem 2. On what floor is the elevator now?

_____

**Interesting Tidbit**

The invention of the safety elevator in 1852 by Elisha Graves Otis, allowed people to travel up and down floors in a building.

# Mixed Review and Test Prep

**5** There were 48 people on the train. Then 12 got off. How many people were left on the train?

**A.** 24　　　　**B.** 36　　　　**C.** 50　　　　**D.** 60

**Up and Down the Number Line**

# Repeat After Me

The graph shows an elevator trip.
Each dot shows a stop during
the trip.

**1** The graph shows a set of changes that
repeat. After how many changes does
the pattern begin to repeat?     _____

**2** What changes are in the pattern
before it starts to repeat?     _____

**3** How many times does the pattern repeat?     _____

**4** What is the net change **each time** the
pattern repeats?     _____

## Mixed Review and Test Prep

**5** On a 100 chart, how far is it from 68 to 100?

**A.** 42          **B.** 40          **C.** 32          **D.** 30

*Use after Investigation 2 (Representing Elevator Trips), Sessions 2 and 3.*

Name _____ Date _____

# Four Little Graphs

Four students drew these graphs that show changes.

**Family Connection**

Students use a graph to describe relative changes as plus, minus, or zero. **Questions you might ask your child:** "How can you recognize a plus change on a graph? A minus change? A change of 0?"

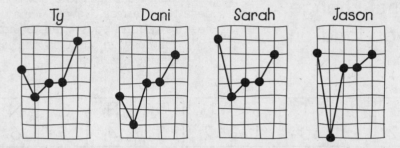

Ty        Dani        Sarah        Jason

**1** Use −, +, or 0 to write the set of changes for each elevator trip.

Ty _____    Dani _____

Sarah _____    Jason _____

**2** How are the graphs the same?

_____

**3** How are the graphs different?

_____

**4** Is the net change −, +, or 0 for each graph?

Ty _____    Dani _____    Sarah _____    Jason _____

# Mixed Review and Test Prep

**5** There are 12 birds in a tree. Then 4 more birds come. How many birds are there now?

**A.** 3          **B.** 12          **C.** 13          **D.** 16

**Up and Down the Number Line**

# You Can Count On It!

For each exercise, start with a counter or a penny on 0. Move the counter to show each net change. Record the letter that you land on.

**Family Connection**

This work prepares students for upcoming class situations in which they create and play their own board games. Previously in the unit, students had been moving up for positive changes and down for negative changes. Now you may need to remind your child to move right for positive changes and left for negative changes.

| O | M | E | U | T | J | T | S | U | T | H | C | N |
|---|---|---|---|---|---|---|---|---|---|---|---|---|
| −6 | −5 | −4 | −3 | −2 | −1 | 0 | 1 | 2 | 3 | 4 | 5 | 6 |

| | | Net Change | Letter |
|---|---|---|---|
| **1** | −2 +1 | −1 | J |
| **2** | −3 0 | −3 | U |
| **3** | +2 −1 | | |
| **4** | +1 +2 | | |
| **5** | +3 +2 | | |
| **6** | 0 −6 | | |
| **7** | −1 +3 | | |

| | | Net Change | Letter |
|---|---|---|---|
| **8** | +1 +5 | | |
| **9** | −3 +3 | | |
| **10** | +2 −4 | | |
| **11** | +3 +1 | | |
| **12** | −2 −2 | | |
| **13** | −2 −3 | | |

Answer the riddle by writing the letters in order below.

How can you tell if there are 5 elephants in the freezer?

__ __ __ __ __   __ __ __ __ __   __ __ __ __ __ !

# Mixed Review and Test Prep

**4** Which does **not** have the same result as 7 + 6?

**A.** 6 + 6 + 1    **B.** 12 + 1    **C.** 7 + 7 − 1    **D.** 14 + 1

Name _____                          Date _____

# Jobs!

Play *Jobs!* Follow
these rules:

**Family Connection**

In class, students are designing and playing their
own board game. On this page, they play **Jobs!**
Try playing the game. Can you make $50 in fewer
moves than it took your child?

- Put a counter on 0.

- Use any of these
  changes to move the counter:
  −3 −2 −1 0 +1 +2 +3

- Try to earn a total of $50 in
  the least number of moves.

- You can do a job only once.

**1** I made these moves:

_____

**2** Add the amount of money
gained or lost on each
move. Be sure it totals $50.

_____

| | |
|---|---|
| Clean attic for $10 | 6 |
| Watch 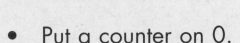, lose $5 | 5 |
| ☺-sit for $15 | 4 |
| Walk 🐕 for $5 | 3 |
| Wash 🚗 for $5 | 2 |
| Talk on ☎, lose $15 | 1 |
| Start | 0 |
| Eat a 🍕, lose $10 | −1 |
| Mow lawn for $10 | −2 |
| Shoot 🏀, lose $5 | −3 |
| Garden for $20 | −4 |
| Play 🏈, lose $15 | −5 |

# Mixed Review and Test Prep

**3** Which does not show the total number
of squares in all?

**A.** 8 + 2          **C.** 2 + 3 + 3

**B.** 4 + 4 + 2      **D.** 2 + 6 + 2

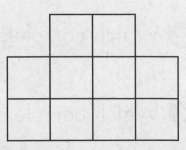

# Batter Up!

Play *Batter Up!*
Follow these rules:

- Put a counter on 0.

- Use any of these changes to move the counter:
  $-3$ $-2$ $-1$ 0 $+1$ $+2$ $+3$

- Use exactly 4 moves to get as many points as you can.

- You can land on each space only once.

**Family Connection**

In class, students played board games that they designed. On this page, they play **Batter Up!** Have your child explain his or her strategy for playing this game. Then try it yourself.

**1** What moves did you make?

_____

**2** How many points did you get?

_____

| | |
|---|---|
| Home run: 4 points | 6 |
| Triple: 3 points | 5 |
| Out: lose 2 points | 4 |
| Foul ball: lose 1 point | 3 |
| Double: 2 points | 2 |
| Strike: lose 1 point | 1 |
| Start | 0 |
| Triple: 3 points | −1 |
| Single: 1 point | −2 |
| Triple play: lose 3 points | −3 |
| Double: 2 points | −4 |
| Home run: 4 points | −5 |

# Mixed Review and Test Prep

**3** Which completes this sentence? $8 + \underline{\phantom{00}} = 12$

**A.** 4　　　**B.** 5　　　**C.** 6　　　**D.** 7

**4** Which completes this sentence? $9 - \underline{\phantom{00}} = 6$

**A.** 4　　　**B.** 3　　　**C.** 2　　　**D.** 1

# HOW Tall?

Here are the heights of some Grade 3 students:

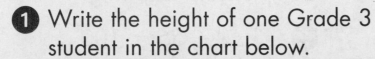

Marcia: 50 inches

Juán: 51 inches

Ricky: 48 inches

Milo: 53 inches

**1** Write the height of one Grade 3 student in the chart below.

| Record Height (Tallest Person) | Height of a Grade 3 Student |
|---|---|
| 107 inches | |

This is what the tallest person in the world would look like next to these Grade 3 students!

**2** What is the difference in inches between the height of the third grader and the height of the tallest person in the world?

_____

**3** Explain the strategy you used to find the difference between the two heights.

_____

_____

## Mixed Review and Test Prep

**4** There were 21 apples on a tree. Seven of them fell off. How many are left on the tree?

**A.** 7          **B.** 14          **C.** 16          **D.** 26

# Hundred Pairs

**1** Connect the pairs of numbers that make 100.

| 37 | 29 |
| 48 | 32 |
| 71 | 73 |
| 81 | 96 |
| 68 | 63 |
| 27 | 52 |
| 4 | 19 |

Complete the following.

**2** _____ + 55 = 100

**3** 15 + _____ = 100

**4** 30 + _____ = 100

**5** _____ + 45 = 100

Find other pairs of numbers that make 100.
Complete the following.

**6** _____ + _____ = 100

**7** _____ + _____ = 100

**8** _____ + _____ = 100

**9** _____ + _____ = 100

**Interesting Tidbit**

Centipedes are thought to have 100 legs. In fact, some centipedes have as few as 30, and others have more than 100!

# Mixed Review and Test Prep

**10** How many people have 2 pets?

**A.** 4          **C.** 2

**B.** 3          **D.** 1

**Class Pets**

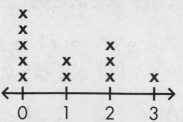

© Pearson Education, Inc. 3

**Combining and Comparing**

# Oldest Animals

These animals lived a
record number of years:

| Animal | Record Ages |
|--------|-------------|
| Parrot | 35 years |
| Monkey | 53 years |
| Alligator | 66 years |
| Eel | 88 years |

**Family Connection**

Students are developing strategies for finding the difference
between two numbers. To give
your child additional practice,
write down the ages of older
members of your family. Then
ask your child to find how many
years it will take for him or her
to reach the same age as each
of these relatives.

**1** How many more years did the oldest
monkey live than the oldest parrot?           _____

**2** How many more years would the
oldest alligator have to have lived to
live as long as the oldest eel?               _____

**3** A young alligator is 9 years old. How
many more years will it need to live
to tie the record for the oldest alligator?   _____

**4** Explain the strategy you used to find
the answer in Problem 3.

---

## Mixed Review and Test Prep

**5** Which does **not** equal 47?

   **A.** 40 − 7     **B.** 50 − 3     **C.** 30 + 17     **D.** 39 + 8

**Combining and Comparing**

# Weighing Toys

Which toy
weighs more?

The _____ is heavier.

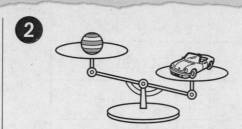

The _____ is heavier.

 The two sides of the balance scale at the right balance. What does this tell you about the weight of the toys?

_____

_____

_____

# Mixed Review and Test Prep

**4** Which shape has 4 corners?

A.    B. 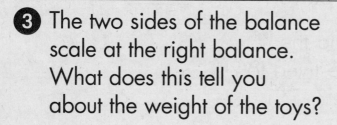   C.    D.

**Combining and Comparing**

# Food for Thought

Complete the chart. Then shade the puzzle pieces with those answers.

**Family Connection**

Students used a pan balance to find the weights of fruits and vegetables before and after a few days of drying out. Ask students to explain why some foods lost weight after sitting out for a day or more.

| | Food | Starting Weight | Second Weight | Difference |
|---|---|---|---|---|
| 1 | Apple slice | 32 paper clips | 26 paper clips | |
| 2 | Kiwi | 53 paper clips | 45 paper clips | |
| 3 | Raisins | 37 paper clips | 37 paper clips | |
| 4 | Cucumber chunk | 30 paper clips | 18 paper clips | |
| 5 | Tomato slice | 27 paper clips | 20 paper clips | |
| 6 | Strawberry | 22 paper clips | 19 paper clips | |

# Mixed Review and Test Prep

**7** Which does **not** equal 100?

**A.** 45 + 55     **B.** 20 + 80     **C.** 30 + 65     **D.** 85 + 15

**Combining and Comparing**

# Marble Grab Bag

Six students took marbles from a bag.
They had a total of 300 marbles.

**Family Connection**

Students are developing a variety of addition strategies. **Questions you might ask your child:** "Did you use the same strategy in Problems 1 and 2?" "What strategy would you use if the six students grabbed 200 marbles?"

**1** Complete the picture to show
one way six students could have
grabbed the marbles.

50

**2** Show a different way six students could
have grabbed the marbles.

**3** Describe the strategy you used to complete
either Problem 1 or Problem 2.

_____

_____

_____

## Mixed Review and Test Prep

**4** Kelly sorted numbers into two groups.
Which of these numbers belongs in
Group A?

| Group A | Group B |
|---------|---------|
| 8, 10, 4, 6 | 9, 13, 3, 7 |

**A.** 1          **B.** 5          **C.** 12          **D.** 15

**Combining and Comparing**

# Coupon Cutting

These coupons are
in a grocery store ad:

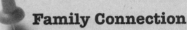
| | | | | |
|---|---|---|---|---|
| **$ .75 OFF!** cereal  | **$.50 off cleaner** | $1.25 off yogurt 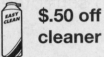 | **20¢ off spaghetti** 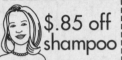 | **eggs 40¢ off** |
| **$1.00 off juice** | **$.45 off pretzels**  | **60¢ off pudding** | **$.85 off shampoo** | **35¢ off butter** |

**1** Find and list coupons that add up to $3.00.

_____

_____

**2** Find and list **three** coupons that add up to $1.50.

_____

_____

**3** Will the savings on cereal, yogurt, and eggs
be more or less than $2.00? Explain.

_____

_____

# Mixed Review and Test Prep

**4** About how many paper clips long is the crayon?

**A.** 4          **B.** 3          **C.** 2          **D.** 1

**Combining and Comparing**

# Fun at the Zoo

A class is going
to the zoo.

**Family Connection**

Students are working with units of time. Make a schedule of your child's evening activities similar to the one below. Ask your child to find the total number of minutes he or she spends on all these activities.

**1** Choose 5 activities and complete the schedule below.
Choose starting times that fit.

Monkey Antics (60 minutes)     Bird House (30 minutes)
Dolphin Show (45 minutes)       Safari Ride (45 minutes)
Penguin Parade (90 minutes)     Lunch (45 minutes)
Petting Zoo (60 minutes)         Gift Shopping (30 minutes)

| Activity | Starting time | How many minutes? |
|---|---|---|
| Bus Ride to Zoo | 9:00 | 45 |
|  | 9:45 |  |
|  |  |  |
|  |  |  |
|  |  |  |
|  |  |  |
| Bus Ride to School |  | 45 |
| Arrive at School |  |  |

**2** How many minutes does the field trip last altogether?

_____

# Mixed Review and Test Prep

**Box Weighing**

**3** How many boxes were weighed?

**A.** 2      **C.** 6

**B.** 4      **D.** 8

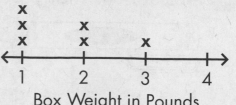

Box Weight in Pounds

**Combining and Comparing**

# Grab Some Clips

Some students recorded the number of paper clips they could hold in each hand.

**Family Connection**

Students are making comparisons and recording information on line plots. Ask your child what type of information he or she can quickly read from a line plot. Also ask your child to explain how he or she determines the total number of students represented in the line plot on this page.

**1** Find the differences.

| Name | Right Hand | Left Hand | Difference |
|------|-----------|-----------|------------|
| Gwen | 56 | 47 | |
| Stefano | 61 | 65 | |
| Nicole | 48 | 52 | |
| Vic | 57 | 49 | |

**2** This line plot shows the differences for the **rest** of the students in the class. Finish the line plot by adding the differences for the students in the chart above.

**Paper Clip Data**

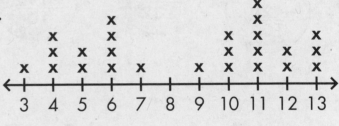

# Mixed Review and Test Prep

**3** Ben made this Venn diagram to sort the students in his class. How many students have both brown hair and blue eyes?

Brown hair      Blue eyes

Ben
Sandy      Sam
Vera   Bill  Benna  Mike      Beth
Keoni  Sal  Andy

**A.** 11          **B.** 6          **C.** 4          **D.** 1

**Combining and Comparing**

# Golf Ball Trivia

**1** Match addition and subtraction problems that show the same situation. Find the ball that's left. The answer to that problem gives the number of dimples on a regulation golf ball!

**Family Connection**

Students are relating addition and subtraction to comparison situations. Ask your child to make up a comparison situation to match one of the golf balls.

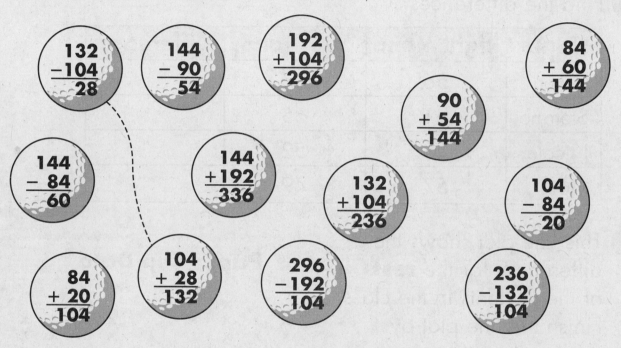

$$\begin{array}{r} 132 \\ -104 \\ \hline 28 \end{array} \qquad \begin{array}{r} 144 \\ -\ 90 \\ \hline 54 \end{array} \qquad \begin{array}{r} 192 \\ +104 \\ \hline 296 \end{array} \qquad \begin{array}{r} 84 \\ +\ 60 \\ \hline 144 \end{array}$$

$$\begin{array}{r} 144 \\ -\ 84 \\ \hline 60 \end{array} \qquad \begin{array}{r} 144 \\ +192 \\ \hline 336 \end{array} \qquad \begin{array}{r} 90 \\ +\ 54 \\ \hline 144 \end{array}$$

$$\begin{array}{r} 132 \\ +104 \\ \hline 236 \end{array} \qquad \begin{array}{r} 104 \\ -\ 84 \\ \hline 20 \end{array}$$

$$\begin{array}{r} 84 \\ +\ 20 \\ \hline 104 \end{array} \qquad \begin{array}{r} 104 \\ +\ 28 \\ \hline 132 \end{array} \qquad \begin{array}{r} 296 \\ -192 \\ \hline 104 \end{array} \qquad \begin{array}{r} 236 \\ -132 \\ \hline 104 \end{array}$$

# Mixed Review and Test Prep

**2** Which animal is about the same length as this string?

├─── 1 inch

**A.** Ant, 1 inch          **C.** Cat, 12 inches

**B.** Hamster, 5 inches          **D.** Snake, 22 inches

## Combining and Comparing

# Pop! Pop! Pop!

The students at Taft
School blew up
balloons for a fun fair.
The balloons came
in bags like this one.

100 balloons

**Family Connection**
Many items, such as tissues,
coffee filters, and notebook paper,
come in sets of one hundred. Find
something around your home that
is sold in hundreds, such as paper.
**Questions you might ask your child:**
"How many sheets of paper would
we have if we had 5 packs of
paper?" "How many sheets would
be left if we used 20 sheets?"

**1** The school had 9 bags of
balloons. Then 8 more
bags arrived. How many
balloons were there in all
the bags?

_____

**2** The students blew up
400 balloons for the
cafeteria. Thirty popped.
How many balloons
were left?

_____

**3** The students used 5 bags
of balloons to decorate the
parking lot. Fifty blew
away. How many balloons
were left?

_____

**4** There were 200 balloons
in the gym. Then the
students put up another 450.
How many balloons were
there in all?

_____

# Mixed Review and Test Prep

**5** Beth jumped three times and then measured
each jump in inches. Her jumps measured
19 inches, 24 inches, and 36 inches. What
is the total length of all of her jumps?

**A.** 79 inches    **B.** 69 inches    **C.** 43 inches    **D.** 24 inches

**Combining and Comparing**

# Related Problems

Solve each set of
related problems.

**Family Connection**

Students are learning to use what they know to help
solve more complex problems. Pick a set and ask your
child to explain how the problems in the set are related. If your child needs help, ask how the numbers
change from one problem to the next.

**1**  $400 + 200 =$ _____

  $401 + 201 =$ _____

  $399 + 198 =$ _____

**2**  $500 - 50 =$ _____

  $500 - 60 =$ _____

  $500 - 62 =$ _____

**3**
| 300 | 298 | 310 |
|-----|-----|-----|
| 300 | 297 | 290 |
| + 300 | + 301 | + 295 |

**4**
| 1000 | 900 | 702 |
|------|-----|-----|
| − 50 | − 50 | − 50 |

**5** Pick one problem set above. Explain how you used
some of the problems in the set to solve others.

_____

_____

_____

# Mixed Review and Test Prep

**6** How far is the shortest path
from the school to the library?

**A.** 1 block   **C.** 3 blocks

**B.** 2 blocks   **D.** 4 blocks

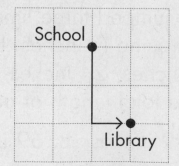

**Combining and Comparing**

# How Many Days?

Use the calendar and the list of special dates to solve the problems.

**Family Connection**

Students are using a calendar to solve problems. Look at a calendar with your child and point out a holiday or event that is coming up shortly. Ask your child to tell you how many more days until the special occasion and then to explain how he or she solved the problem.

**1** If today is Jenn's birthday, how many days is it until Max's birthday?

_____

**2** If today is the Bake Sale, how many days is it until the Field Trip?

_____

**3** Tim's art class begins on May 10, which is three weeks from today. What is today's date?

_____

**4** The Art Show is one week after the Science Fair. What is the date of the Art Show?

_____

| April 8: Jenn's Birthday |
| April 22: Bake Sale |
| April 30: Max's Birthday |
| May 13: Field Trip |
| May 23: Science Fair |

### April

| S | M | T | W | T | F | S |
|---|---|---|---|---|---|---|
|   |   |   |   |   | 1 | 2 |
| 3 | 4 | 5 | 6 | 7 | 8 | 9 |
| 10 | 11 | 12 | 13 | 14 | 15 | 16 |
| 17 | 18 | 19 | 20 | 21 | 22 | 23 |
| 24 | 25 | 26 | 27 | 28 | 29 | 30 |

### May

| S | M | T | W | T | F | S |
|---|---|---|---|---|---|---|
| 1 | 2 | 3 | 4 | 5 | 6 | 7 |
| 8 | 9 | 10 | 11 | 12 | 13 | 14 |
| 15 | 16 | 17 | 18 | 19 | 20 | 21 |
| 22 | 23 | 24 | 25 | 26 | 27 | 28 |
| 29 | 30 | 31 |   |   |   |   |

## Mixed Review and Test Prep

**5** Which number is between 150 and 200?

**A.** 202      **B.** 177      **C.** 145      **D.** 127

**Combining and Comparing**

# Vacation Days

Gina's mom usually works
Monday through Friday.
She is planning to take some
vacation days from June 14
through June 18, July 5
through July 9, and
August 16 through August 20.

**Family Connection**

Students continue to solve calendar problems. Pose
a similar situation about the summer months and
have your child use a calendar to solve the problem.

**1** During June, July, and August,
will Gina's mom have more
days off or more days at work?
Explain how you found
your answer.

_____

_____

_____

_____

| June | | | | | | |
|---|---|---|---|---|---|---|
| **S** | **M** | **T** | **W** | **T** | **F** | **S** |
|  | | 1 | 2 | 3 | 4 | 5 |
| 6 | 7 | 8 | 9 | 10 | 11 | 12 |
| 13 | 14 | 15 | 16 | 17 | 18 | 19 |
| 20 | 21 | 22 | 23 | 24 | 25 | 26 |
| 27 | 28 | 29 | 30 | | | |

| July | | | | | | |
|---|---|---|---|---|---|---|
| **S** | **M** | **T** | **W** | **T** | **F** | **S** |
| | | | | 1 | 2 | 3 |
| 4 | 5 | 6 | 7 | 8 | 9 | 10 |
| 11 | 12 | 13 | 14 | 15 | 16 | 17 |
| 18 | 19 | 20 | 21 | 22 | 23 | 24 |
| 25 | 26 | 27 | 28 | 29 | 30 | 31 |

| August | | | | | | |
|---|---|---|---|---|---|---|
| **S** | **M** | **T** | **W** | **T** | **F** | **S** |
| 1 | 2 | 3 | 4 | 5 | 6 | 7 |
| 8 | 9 | 10 | 11 | 12 | 13 | 14 |
| 15 | 16 | 17 | 18 | 19 | 20 | 21 |
| 22 | 23 | 24 | 25 | 26 | 27 | 28 |
| 29 | 30 | 31 | | | | |

# Mixed Review and Test Prep

**2** Ned described a path he
walked around his house.
How many steps did he walk?

**A.** 13 steps     **C.** 43 steps

**B.** 33 steps     **D.** 48 steps

I walked 15 steps,
and then turned right.
I walked 28 more steps
and turned right into
my house.

**Combining and Comparing**

# Time Travel

A year is the number of days it takes a planet to travel around the sun. The diagram shows the number of days in a year for four planets.

**Family Connection**
Students continue comparing data to solve problems. You and your child might enjoy investigating the lengths of the years on other planets and comparing them to the length of a year on Earth. You might also want to help your child research the concept of leap years.

**1** What is the difference between the number of days in the longest year shown here and the number of days in the shortest year?

_____

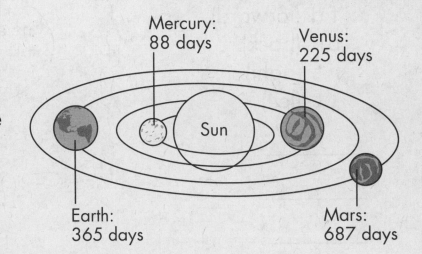

Mercury:
88 days

Venus:
225 days

Sun

Earth:
365 days

Mars:
687 days

**2** What is the difference between the number of days in a year on Mars and the number of days in a year on Earth?

_____

# Mixed Review and Test Prep

**3** Which does **not** equal 76?

    **A.** 50 + 36          **C.** 26 + 50

    **B.** 100 − 24        **D.** 25 + 51

# Follow the Path

**1** Write a set of commands to follow the path shown. Each footprint is a step.

Choose from these commands:
- f d (forward)
- b k (back)
- r t (right)
- l t (left)

_____

_____

_____

_____

_____

**Family Connection**

Students have been writing commands that give directions for following a path. The commands tell how to move or turn. **Questions you might ask your child:** "How did you decide when to use the command fd?" "When would you use the command lt 90?"

# Mixed Review and Test Prep

**2** Tim made a rectangle with 3 rows of tiles and 2 tiles in each row. Which of these rectangles did Tim make?

**A.**      **B.**      **C.**      **D.**

**Turtle Paths**

# Where Am I?

**1** Draw a path following the commands. REMEMBER: The dots are 10 steps apart.

**Family Connection**
Students continue to write and follow commands to make a path. Ask your child to write commands to get from Home on this sheet to another destination; then follow the commands together to check the path.

Start at Home.
fd 20
rt 90
fd 40
lt 90
fd 50
rt 90
fd 30

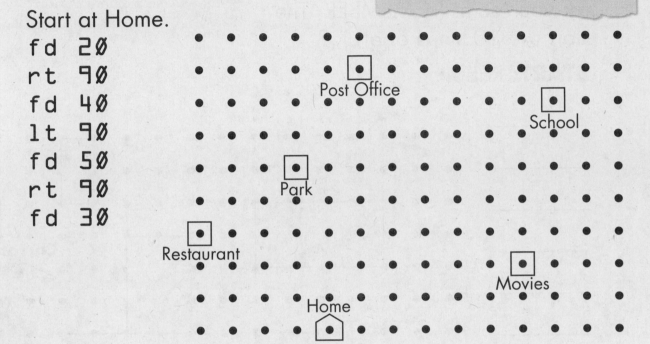

**2** Where did you end? _____

# Mixed Review and Test Prep

**3** Ben has 2 dogs and a cat. He wants to add his data to the graph his friends made. Above which number should he place an **X** on the graph?

**How many pets do you have?**

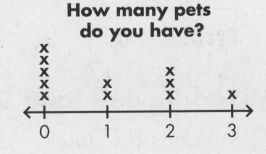

**A.** 0          **C.** 2

**B.** 1          **D.** 3

# Get the Carrot

**1** Draw the shortest path from the rabbit to the carrot. Go around each 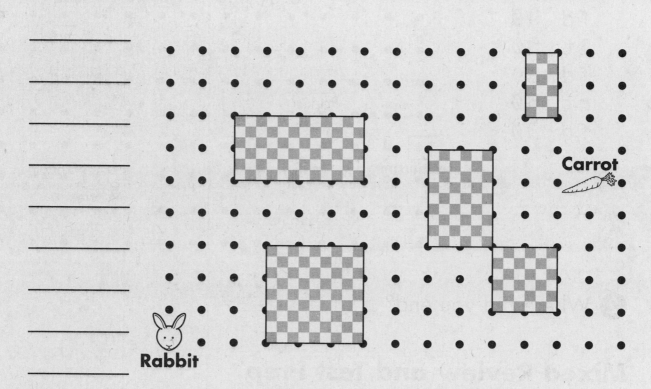. Write the commands for your path. (REMEMBER: The dots are 10 steps apart.)

**START:** Rabbit

_____

_____

_____

_____

_____

_____

_____

_____

_____

_____

_____

**END:** Carrot

# Mixed Review and Test Prep

**2** Which is a square?

A. ▭    B. ☐    C. △    D. ☐

**Turtle Paths**

# Back to Start

Look at the commands used to get from Start to House.

**Family Connection**

Students have been working on computers using Geo-Logo commands. They use mathematical processes such as addition to combine commands. Ask your child to explain how he or she combined commands in this activity.

**1** Write commands to return from the House to Start. **Combine commands** if you can.
(REMEMBER: The dots are 10 steps apart.)

| Start to House | House to Start |
|---|---|
| fd 30 | _____ |
| fd 10 | _____ |
| fd 20 | _____ |
| rt 90 | _____ |
| fd 10 | _____ |
| fd 30 | _____ |

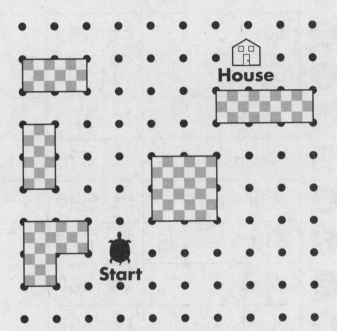

# Mixed Review and Test Prep

**2** Which shows $\frac{1}{2}$ shaded?

A.    B.    C.    D.

**3** Which shows $\frac{1}{3}$ shaded?

A.    B.    C.    D.

Name _____                          Date _____

# Which Direction?

Use the compass
to find the direction
after the turn.

**Family Connection**

Students have been exploring turns as a change in
orientation by acting out the turns. Have your child
stand facing north and then make a turn of 90° to
the left. Have your child tell you in which direction
he or she is now facing. (West)

| | Start Facing | Turn | End Facing |
|---|---|---|---|
| 1 | North | rt 90 | |
| 2 | South | rt 180 | |
| 3 | East | lt 90 | |
| 4 | West | lt 180 | |
| 5 | North | rt 270 | |
| 6 | South | rt 360 | |
| 7 | East | lt 270 | |
| 8 | West | lt 360 | |
| 9 | North | lt 180 | |
| 10 | South | rt 270 | |

**Interesting Tidbit**

A compass helps you
find the direction in
which you are heading.
A compass works using
magnets. Earth has
two magnetic poles
near the North and
South poles. A needle
that is magnetized
continually rotates to
the north-south position.

# Mixed Review and Test Prep

**11** Which figure is shaded $\frac{1}{2}$ black?

A.    B. 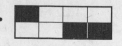   C.    D.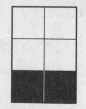

# Turtle Turns

Draw an arrow from the center of the Turtle Turner pointing in the direction that the turtle would be facing after the turn.

**Family Connection**
Students use degrees to estimate and measure turns, understanding that there are 360° in a full turn, 180° in a half turn, and 90° in a quarter turn. Ask your child to show you how he or she would turn to show 180° and to show 90°.

**1** rt 60

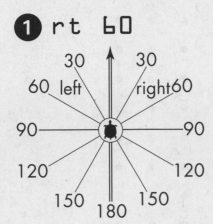

**2** lt 120

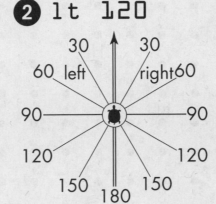

**3** rt 150

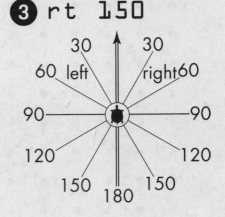

Estimate the turn the turtle would need to make to get ready to draw the dotted line on the path.

**4**

**5**

**6**

_____        _____        _____

# Mixed Review and Test Prep

**7** Which is not a way to show 12?

    **A.** $6 + 6$    **B.** $15 - 3$    **C.** $2 + 3 + 7$    **D.** $14 - 5$

**Turtle Paths**

# Connect the Dots

**1** Connect the dots in order to make each of these words:

**Family Connection**

Students use the definition of a triangle (closed figure with three straight sides and three corners) to decide which figures are triangles. Ask your child to draw three different triangles, and then to use the definition to explain why each drawing is a triangle.

ROAR    KNOCK    LET    HIGH    SUMS    BED

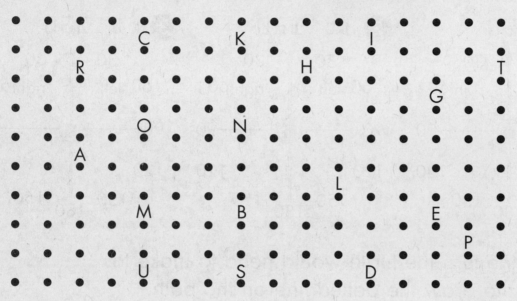

**2** Circle the shapes that are triangles.

**3** Explain why the shapes you circled are triangles.

_____

_____

# Mixed Review and Test Prep

**4** Keith built this model with blocks. There are no hidden blocks. How many blocks did he use?

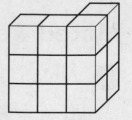

**A.** 15        **B.** 12        **C.** 9        **D.** 6

**Turtle Paths**

# Triangle Hunt

**1** Shade each equilateral triangle below. You should find 10 of them.

**Family Connection**

Students have been working on computers using Geo-Logo commands to make equilateral triangles. Ask your child to describe an equilateral triangle and to tell how he or she knew which triangles shown were not equilateral triangles.

# Mixed Review and Test Prep

**2** How many students were absent 4 or more times?

A. 2          C. 5

B. 3          D. 8

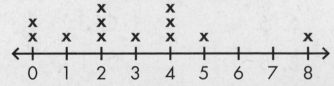

**How many times were you absent last year?**

# Finish the Figure

Write the commands for the turtle to finish each figure. Make the shortest closed path possible.

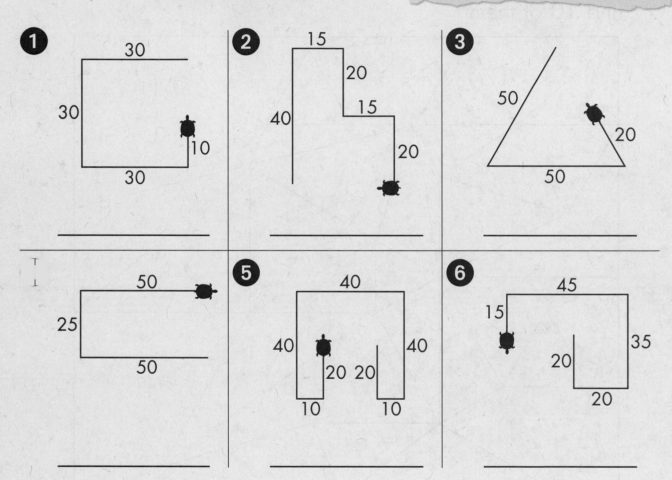

# Mixed Review and Test Prep

How many triangles would you need to cover the larger shape?

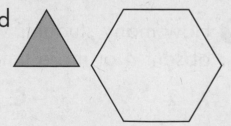

**A.** 6          **C.** 3

**B.** 5          **D.** 1

Name _____      Date _____

**Turtle Paths**

# What's Missing?

Find the missing measure
in each figure. Explain
how you found it.

**Family Connection**

Students continue to develop strategies to find
missing lengths. Discuss your child's explanations
for the exercises. Then ask your child to draw a
figure that has a missing measure for you to solve.

**❶**

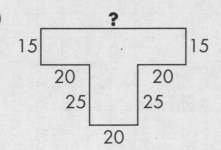

**❷**

**❸**

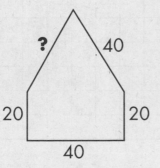

_____

_____

_____

_____

_____

_____

_____

_____

_____

_____

_____

_____

# Mixed Review and Test Prep

**❹** Which shape fits the rule?
    **Rule:** The shapes have 4 sides.
        None of the sides are the same length.

**A.** ▢      **B.** ◣      **C.** ▱      **D.** ▭

© Pearson Education, Inc. 3

*Use after Investigation 2 (Turns in Paths), Sessions 5 and 6.*   **125**

# Paths and Perimeters

**1** Draw 6 different closed paths that each have a perimeter of 20. They may be rectangles or other closed paths. Label the length of each side.

The side of each of these little squares has a length of 1.

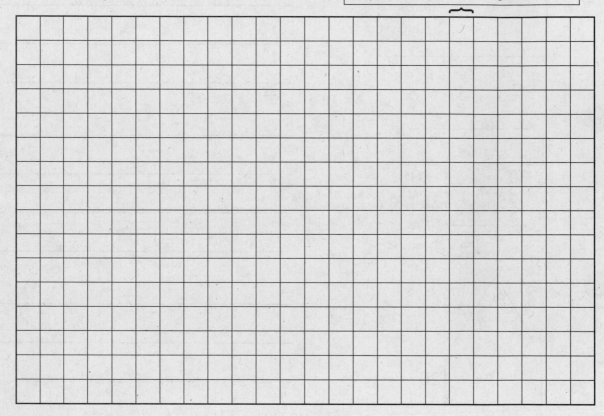

# Mixed Review and Test Prep

**2** This design has 12 tiles, and $\frac{1}{3}$ of the tiles are black. How many tiles are black?

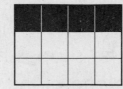

**A.** 1          **B.** 3          **C.** 4          **D.** 8

© Pearson Education, Inc. **3**

**Turtle Paths**

# Completing Rectangles

The perimeter and length of one side of a rectangle are given. Write the lengths of the other sides. Draw a sketch to help.

**Family Connection**

Students use their knowledge of the properties of rectangles to draw a rectangle when given the length of one side and the perimeter. Ask your child to explain how he or she found the lengths of the sides of the rectangles in this activity.

**1** Perimeter: 100
Length of a side: 30

_____

**2** Perimeter: 180
Length of a side: 40

_____

**3** Perimeter: 200
Length of a side: 75

_____

**4** Perimeter: 150
Length of a side: 30

_____

# Mixed Review and Test Prep

**5** Brandon has to read 25 pages for homework. He has already read 12 pages. How many pages does Brandon have left to read?

    **A.** 37        **B.** 13        **C.** 12        **D.** 3

**Turtle Paths**

# Building Shapes

Aaron combined two of these three shapes to make a new shape:

**Family Connection**

Students are beginning a project in class in which they will be applying their knowledge of paths and perimeter to a number of shapes. Ask your child to build a new shape using all three figures and then to find its perimeter.

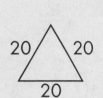
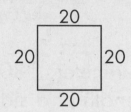
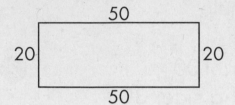

Here's the new shape Aaron made:

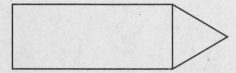

**1** What is the perimeter of Aaron's new shape? _____

_____

**2** Combine the rectangle and the square. Draw the new shape. Find the perimeter.

_____

_____

**3** Combine the square and the triangle. Draw the new shape. Find the perimeter.

_____

_____

# Mixed Review and Test Prep

**4** Sue and her brother are sharing the pinecones they collect. Which number of pinecones **cannot** be shared equally?

**A.** 2          **B.** 8          **C.** 12          **D.** 15

**Turtle Paths**

# Making Shapes

Draw a sketch of the given shape. Label the length of each side.

**Family Connection**

Sketching a geometric figure is an important tool for solving a variety of problems. Ask your child to explain his or her strategy for drawing each of the shapes on this page.

**1** Square with a perimeter of 80

**2** Equilateral triangle with a perimeter of 90

**3** Rectangle with a perimeter of 120

**4** Square with a perimeter of 160

**5** Equilateral triangle with a perimeter of 150

**6** Rectangle with a perimeter of 180

# Mixed Review and Test Prep

**7** $46 - \boxed{\phantom{0}} = 28$

**A.** 32      **B.** 28      **C.** 18      **D.** 15

# Which Goes with Which?

Each set of commands will draw
a shape. Write the letter of the
matching shape for each set
of commands.

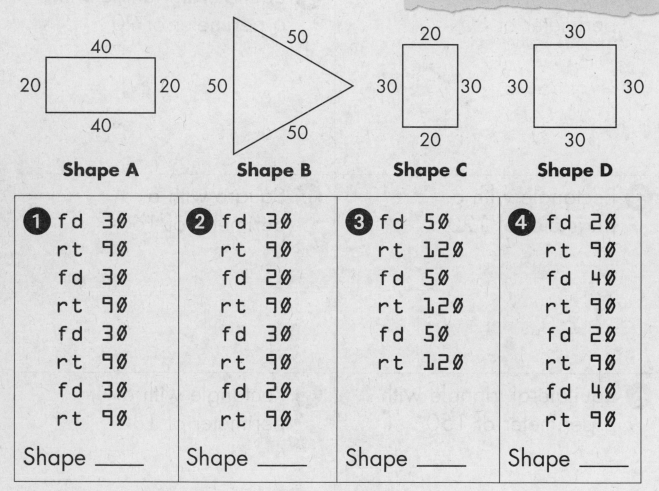

**Shape A**  **Shape B**  **Shape C**  **Shape D**

❶ fd 30
rt 90
fd 30
rt 90
fd 30
rt 90
fd 30
rt 90

Shape ____

❷ fd 30
rt 90
fd 20
rt 90
fd 30
rt 90
fd 20
rt 90

Shape ____

❸ fd 50
rt 120
fd 50
rt 120
fd 50
rt 120

Shape ____

❹ fd 20
rt 90
fd 40
rt 90
fd 20
rt 90
fd 40
rt 90

Shape ____

# Mixed Review and Test Prep

❺ Marcy wants to shade one-half of
the large rectangle. How many
tiles should she shade?

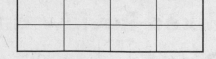

**A.** 2          **B.** 4          **C.** 8          **D.** 10

**Turtle Paths**

# Making Faces

**1** Greg is drawing a robot on the computer. Choose a head from the choices below to complete the robot. Draw it on the robot. Then write the commands to make that head.

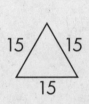 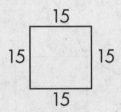 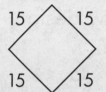

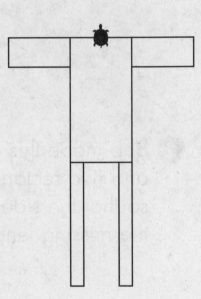

_____    _____

_____    _____

_____    _____

_____    _____

# Mixed Review and Test Prep

**2** The paper is folded in half. If you cut along the dotted line, what shape will you see when you unfold the paper?

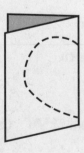

**A.** heart          **C.** diamond

**B.** rectangle      **D.** circle

# Growing and Shrinking Designs

Tina and Bob are making designs
on the computer.

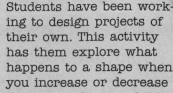

**Family Connection**
Students have been working to design projects of their own. This activity has them explore what happens to a shape when you increase or decrease the size. Ask your child to explain his or her strategy for finding the lengths in the new shapes.

**1** Tina made this design using equilateral
triangles and a square. She wants to
change the design so that the sides
are twice as long. Write the missing
lengths in the new design.

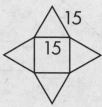

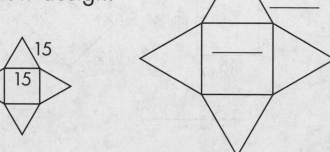

**2** Bob made this design using an equilateral triangle
and two rectangles. He wants to change the design
so that the sides are half as long. Write
the missing lengths in the new design.

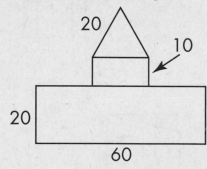

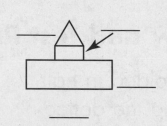

# Mixed Review and Test Prep

**3** Find the missing number. $35 + \boxed{\phantom{x}} = 60$

**A.** 25          **B.** 23          **C.** 20          **D.** 15

**Fair Shares**

# Sharing with Friends

**1** Jim cut this pizza into 8 pieces. Will 8 people get an equal share? Why or why not?

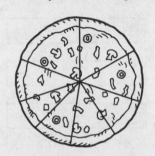

**2** Draw lines to show how 4 people can share this granola bar equally.

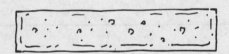

Each person gets _____.

**3** Draw lines to show how 6 people can share this cornbread equally.

Each person gets _____.

# Mixed Review and Test Prep

**4** Which activity is an 8-year-old child most likely to do at 9:00 P.M.?

**A.** Eat breakfast

**C.** Go to school

**B.** Go to bed

**D.** Ride a bike

**Fair Shares**

# Put Them in Order!

Look at the shaded part of each shape. Write the fractions in order from **smallest** to **largest.**

**Family Connection**

Students are learning about the relative sizes of various fractions. Your child has ordered models of fractions from least to greatest. Ask your child to explain how he or she ordered the three fractions in Exercise 1.

**1** | **2** | **3**

_____ | _____ | _____

**1** Explain how you ordered the fractions in Exercise 1.

_____

_____

_____

# Mixed Review and Test Prep

**2** Which activity did Jane and Lydia do at the same time?

A. Wake up

B. Read

C. Ride bike

D. Play

| Jane | | Lydia | |
|------|--------|------|--------|
| Time | Activity | Time | Activity |
| 8:00 | Wake up | 8:00 | Sleep |
| 9:00 | Ride bike | 9:00 | Wake up |
| 10:00 | Read | 10:00 | Read |
| 11:00 | Play | 11:00 | Ride bike |

**Fair Shares**

# Sharing Stories

Show how to share each group of items equally. Draw what each person gets. Then write the amount.

**Family Connection**

Students are learning to share a group of items equally among a number of people. They first identify how many whole items each person would get, and then they divide the rest by using fractional parts.

**1** Three friends share 4 sheets of construction paper.


Each person gets _____.

**2** Four friends share 6 cookies.



Each person gets _____.

# Mixed Review and Test Prep

**3** George asked his friends to name their favorite color. How many friends did he survey?

| Yellow   IIII | Blue   卌 III | Red   卌 III |
|---------------|--------------|-------------|

**A.** 6           **B.** 8           **C.** 17           **D.** 20

# Naming Fractions

Write a fraction or a mixed number for the shaded part.

**Family Connection**
Students are becoming familiar with grouping fractions and naming equal fractions. They are learning that fractions can be combined with whole numbers.

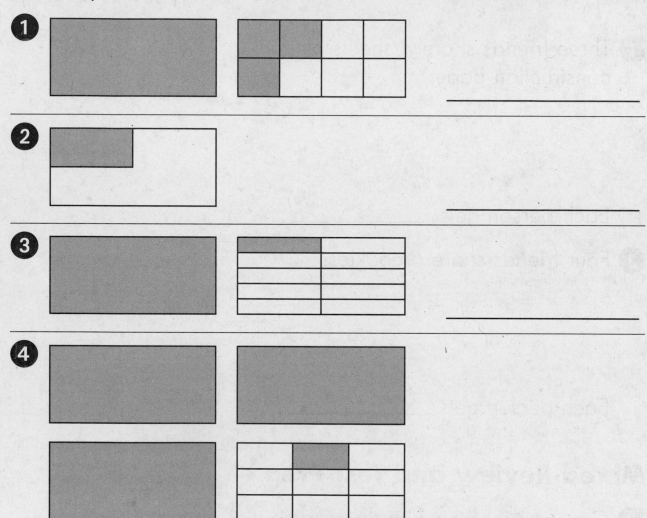

1 _____

2 _____

3 _____

4 _____

# Mixed Review and Test Prep

5 Brittany asked fifteen people if they like to play tag. Nine people said, "YES!" How many people said "NO"?

**A.** 15          **B.** 9          **C.** 6          **D.** 0

**Fair Shares**

# Many Ways to Make a Whole

Write the correct fraction on each piece. Then write a number sentence to show what fractions make the whole.

**Family Connection**
Students are working with equivalent fractions, focusing especially on the relationships among halves, thirds, and sixths.

**1**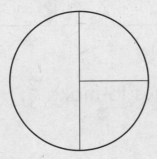

_____

**2**

_____

**3**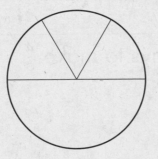

_____

**4**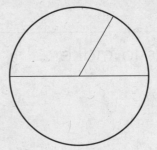

_____

# Mixed Review and Test Prep

**5** How are these shapes the same?

**A.** They are rectangles.

**B.** They have 5 sides.

**C.** They have curved sides.

**D.** They have 4 corners.

**Fair Shares**

# Many Ways to Make a Part

Use these shapes.

**Family Connection**
Students are learning to find different parts of a whole and to use fractions to show how to record these parts.

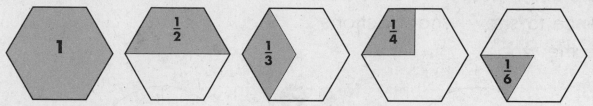

Show different ways to make the amount.

**1** Ways to make $\frac{1}{2}$:

**2** Ways to make $\frac{2}{3}$:

**3** Ways to make $\frac{3}{4}$:

**4** Ways to make $\frac{4}{6}$:

# Mixed Review and Test Prep

**5** How many children wear red or white tennis shoes?

A. 5
C. 12
B. 11
D. 16

**Shoe Color**

| Color | Red | Blue | White |
|---|---|---|---|
| Children | 卌 | 卌 II | 卌 卌 I |

**Fair Shares**

# Who Gets More?

Today the students in Room 222 have blueberry muffins to share. Each group gets 8 muffins to share equally.

### Family Connection

Students are working with fractions and mixed numbers to compare equal shares. Ask your child how three people can share seven pizzas with each person receiving the same share. Then ask your child to compare this situation to four people sharing seven pizzas. Have your child explain the strategy he or she uses to solve the problem.

**1** **Group A:** 6 students share 8 muffins.
**Group B:** 5 students share 8 muffins.

Who gets the larger share?
Tell how you decided. Use words **and** drawings.

_____

_____

**2** Sam thinks that $1\frac{1}{2}$ is a smaller share than $1\frac{1}{5}$. Which share do you think is smaller? Is Sam right or wrong? Explain how you know.

### Interesting Tidbit

Did you know that ancient Egyptians used fractions? This picture shows how they wrote $\frac{1}{3}$.

_____

_____

# Mixed Review and Test Prep

**3** How many more students chose math than chose reading?

**Favorite Subject**

Reading ☐☐☐
Math ☐☐☐☐☐
History ☐☐
Science ☐☐☐☐☐

Each ☐ equals 1 student

**A.** 4          **B.** 3          **C.** 2          **D.** 0

# Equal Fractions

**1** Draw a line to match equal fractions.

**Family Connection**

Students are learning to identify fractional parts, name equivalent fractions, and add and subtract fractions.

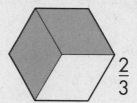
$\frac{2}{3}$

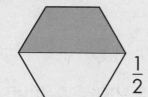
$\frac{1}{2}$

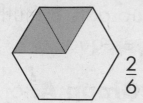
$\frac{2}{6}$

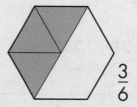
$\frac{3}{6}$

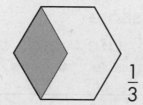
$\frac{1}{3}$

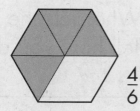
$\frac{4}{6}$

**2** How much of each shape is **not** shaded?

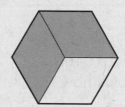 _____

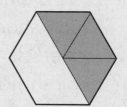 _____

# Mixed Review and Test Prep

**3** There are 28 students in the class. Nine students have brown eyes. How many students do **not** have brown eyes?

**A.** 9          **B.** 19          **C.** 21          **D.** 37

**Fair Shares**

# How Many Sandwiches?

**Family Connection**
Students are focusing on putting pieces together to make wholes, and looking for number patterns to solve problems. After your child has completed the table in Exercise 3, have him or her draw a picture to support each answer.

**1** Four people each get $1\frac{1}{4}$ sandwiches. How many sandwiches are there in all? Draw a picture and tell how many.

_____ sandwiches in all

**2** Draw a picture to show how 3 people could each have $2\frac{2}{3}$ sandwiches. Tell how many sandwiches in all.

_____ sandwiches in all

**3** Complete the tables.

| Share = $2\frac{1}{3}$ | |
|---|---|
| People | Sandwiches |
| 3 | |
| | 14 |

| Share = $\frac{3}{4}$ | |
|---|---|
| People | Sandwiches |
| | 6 |
| 4 | |

# Mixed Review and Test Prep

**4** There are 28 students in the class. If 22 students are present, how many are absent?

**A.** 3          **B.** 4          **C.** 5          **D.** 6

**Fair Shares**

# Portion Puzzles

Solve each problem. Then connect the dots in the order of your answers.

**1** How many pies are needed for 12 people to each have $\frac{1}{6}$ of a pie? _____

How many pizzas are needed for 24 people to each have $\frac{1}{4}$ of a pizza? _____

**3** How many breakfast bars are needed for 5 people to each have $1\frac{3}{5}$ bars? _____

**4** How many sheets of paper are needed for 4 people to each have $3\frac{1}{4}$ sheets? _____

How many blocks of clay are needed for 6 people to each have $2\frac{1}{3}$ blocks? _____

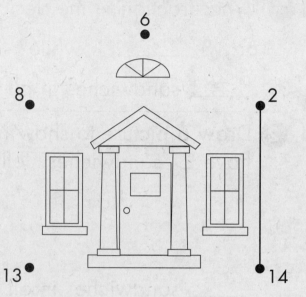

# Mixed Review and Test Prep

**6** Each number in the box fits a mystery rule. Which rule is it?

| 2 | 10 |
|---|---|
| **6** | **20** |

**A.** Even numbers

**C.** Odd numbers

**B.** Numbers greater than 5

**D.** Number less than 10

**Fair Shares**

# Fraction Designs

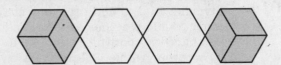

**Family Connection**
Students are learning to describe complex designs using fractions. Ask your child to create a design that is $\frac{1}{4}$ red. **Questions you might ask your child:** "How do you know that $\frac{1}{4}$ of your design is red? If $\frac{1}{4}$ of the design is red, what part of the design is not red?"

**1** What fraction of the design is ...

gray? _____        white? _____

**2** Explain how you found your answers in Exercise 1.

_____

_____

_____

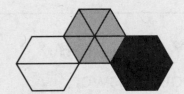

**3** What fraction of the design is ...

gray? _____        white? _____        black? _____

## Mixed Review and Test Prep

**4** Which statement could **not** be made about one of these shapes?

**A.** It has 4 sides.        **C.** It has 4 corners.

**B.** It has equal sides.        **D.** It has 3 sides.

**Fair Shares**

# How Can We Share?

**1** Circle the object if you can share it by splitting it into parts. Draw an **X** over the object if you **cannot** share it by splitting.

**Family Connection**

Students are investigating the relationship between fractions and division. In this activity, your child must decide whether an object can be shared by cutting it into parts, or whether whole objects must be shared. Point out objects around your home that can and cannot be cut into parts, such as a sandwich and a kitchen appliance.

**2** How can 6 people share 8 hot dogs? You may draw a picture to help you. Then explain your answer.

_____

_____

**3** How can 6 people share 8 pencils? You may draw a picture to help you. Then explain your answer.

_____

_____

# Mixed Review and Test Prep

**4** Which expression below shows 25 + 12?

    **A.** 25 + 10 + 2       **C.** 20 + 5 + 10

    **B.** 20 + 10 + 2       **D.** 25 − 10 + 2

**Fair Shares**

# Fraction and Decimal Pairs

**Family Connection**
Students are relating monetary notation to decimal notation on the calculator. They are also learning about decimal and fraction equivalents.

**1** If 4 people share $6.00, each person gets $1\frac{1}{2}$ dollars, or 1.5 dollars. Write this amount using a dollar sign and a decimal point. _____

**2** Ben, Joseph, Carly, and Cindy earned a total of $5.00 for helping Mr. Johnson clean his yard. How much of the money should each person receive?

_____

**3** Complete the table.

| Fractions | $\frac{1}{4}$ | | $\frac{3}{4}$ | $1\frac{1}{2}$ |
|---|---|---|---|---|
| Decimals | | 0.5 | | |

**4** Explain why these two amounts are equal:

$$2.25 \quad = \quad 2\frac{1}{4}$$

_____

_____

# Mixed Review and Test Prep

**5** Which number expression can you use to solve this problem?

The pet store sold 12 dogs and 17 cats. How many cats and dogs were sold in all?

**A.** $12 + 17$  **B.** $17 - 12$  **C.** $29 - 12$  **D.** $17 + 10$

# Sharing Large Quantities

Use words, numbers, or pictures
to solve each problem.

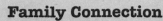

**1** Suppose 9 people share 45 cookies.
What fraction of the cookies will each
person receive? How many cookies
will each person receive?

_____

**2** Find $\frac{1}{4}$ of 28 crayons so that 4 children
can share the crayons equally.

_____

**3** Find $\frac{1}{5}$ of 32 paper clips to show how
many paper clips each of 5 students could have.

_____

_____

# Mixed Review and Test Prep

**4** Greg tried these ways to solve $44 - 19$.
Which way will **not** work?

A. $44 - 20 = 24; \ 24 + 1 = $ _____

B. $40 - 10 = 30; \ 30 - 9 = $ _____

C. $44 - 10 = 34; \ 34 - 9 = $ _____

D. $45 - 20 = $ _____

Name Date

Exploring Solids and Boxes

# Which One Does Not Belong?

Circle the shape that does **not** belong. Then explain how you made your choice.

**Family Connection**

Students are learning to identify important properties of geometric shapes. To practice with your child, display objects from your home, such as a cereal box and a soup can. Ask your child to tell some characteristics about each object.

**1**

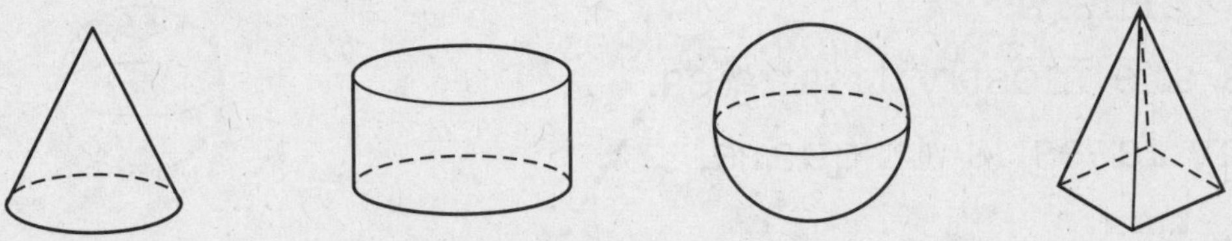

**2**

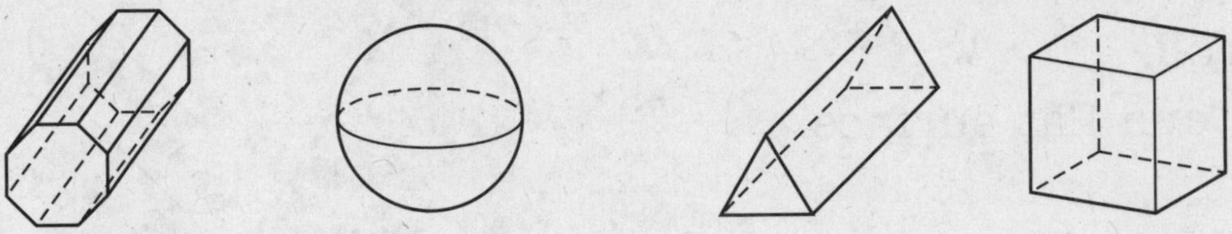

**3**

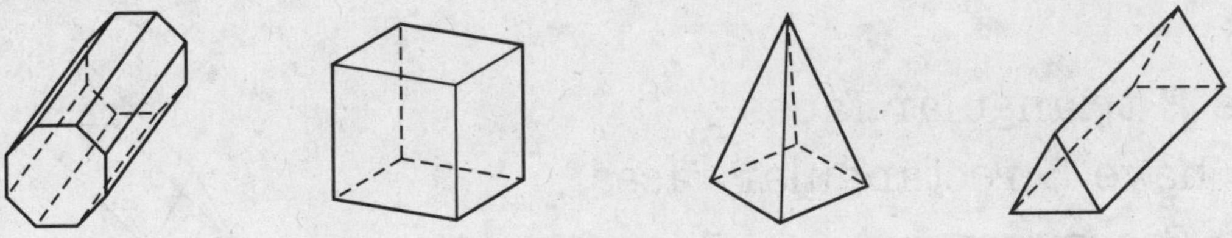

## Mixed Review and Test Prep

Carol has 18 markers. Five markers are blue. How many markers are **not** blue?

**4** Which of the following can you use to solve the story problem?

**A.** 18 + 5 **B.** 18 − 5 **C.** 18 − 18 **D.** 18 + 0

# Mystery Shapes

Draw a line to connect the description to its matching shape.

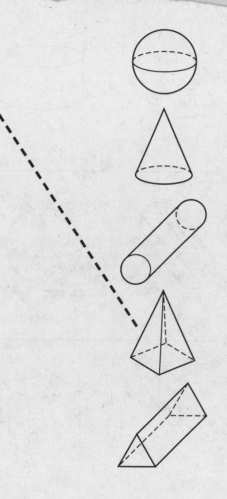

I have 5 corners.
My faces are mostly triangles.
One of my faces is a square.

My surface is curved.
I have no flat surfaces.

**3** I can roll.
I have one flat surface.

I look like a can.
I can roll.
I have two flat surfaces.

I have 2 triangular faces.
I also have 3 rectangular faces.
I have 6 corners.

# Mixed Review and Test Prep

**6** How many blue T-shirts were sold on May 4 and May 5?

A. 34      C. 60

B. 53      D. 94

| T-Shirt Sales | | | |
| --- | --- | --- | --- |
| Date | Blue | Red | Total |
| May 3 | 28 | 20 | 48 |
| May 4 | 29 | 12 | 41 |
| May 5 | 31 | 22 | 53 |

Name _____  Date _____

# How Many Sides and Corners?

Write the number of sides and corners for each shape.

**Family Connection**

Students are building shapes, such as squares, triangles, and rectangles, and identifying the number of sides and corners for each shape. You might want to draw a polygon having more than 4 sides and ask your child if the observation he or she made in Exercise 5 holds true for this new polygon.

**1**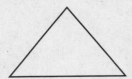

Sides: ____ Corners: ____

**2**

Sides: ____ Corners: ____

**3**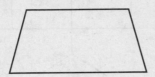

Sides: ____ Corners: ____

**4**

Sides: ____ Corners: ____

**5** What do you notice about the number of sides and the number of corners for each shape?

_____

# Mixed Review and Test Prep

**6** Four students made cube towers to show how many pennies they each have. How many pennies do they have in all?

  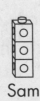

Jan   Paul   Sam   Tia

**A.** 19          **B.** 16          **C.** 14          **D.** 7

**Exploring Solids and Boxes**

# Stained-Glass Window

This stained-glass window has 12 triangles, 8 squares, and 16 rectangles.

**Family Connection**

Students are investigating the properties of triangles, squares, and rectangles. Ask your child to explain why some of these shapes are not triangles, squares, or rectangles. Look for stained-glass windows in your community. See if your child can find any familiar polygons in them.

**1** Color the triangles red, the squares blue, and the rectangles (that aren't squares) green.

**2** Color the other shapes in other colors if you like.

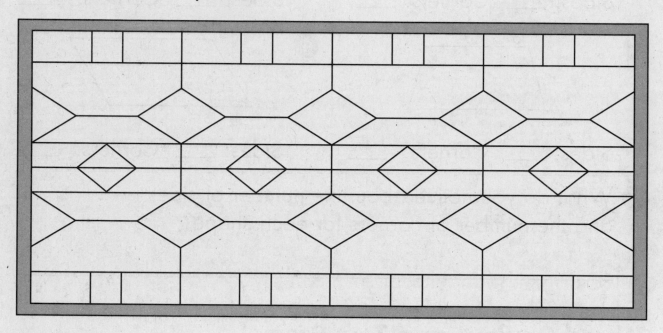

# Mixed Review and Test Prep

**3** Margie has 2 quarters, 2 dimes, and 1 nickel. How much money does Margie have?

**A.** 40¢      **B.** 65¢      **C.** 75¢      **D.** 80¢

**Exploring Solids and Boxes**

# Comparing Solids

Use the solids to answer each question.

**Family Connection**

Students are learning to identify the faces, edges, and corners of 3-dimensional solids. To give your child more practice, select objects from home, such as cereal, cracker, or tissue boxes. Ask your child to tell how many faces, edges, and corners each object has.

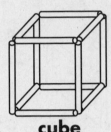

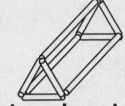

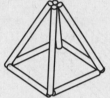

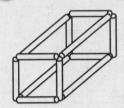

**cube**　　**triangular prism**　　**square pyramid**　　**rectangular prism**

**1** Which figures have exactly 6 faces?

_____

**2** Which figure has exactly 2 triangular faces?

_____

**3** Which figure has exactly 5 corners and 8 edges?

_____

**4** Look at the triangular prism. Tell how many faces, edges, and corners it has.

Faces _____　　　Edges _____　　　Corners _____

## Mixed Review and Test Prep

**5** Which number combination does **not** make 128?

**A.** 100 + 20 + 8　　　　　**C.** 50 + 50 + 8

**B.** 99 + 21 + 8　　　　　**D.** 80 + 40 + 8

# Straw Structures

Gwen built these
polyhedra using straws.

**Family Connection**

Students are learning how to build figures called
polyhedra, three-dimensional figures with all flat
faces. Learning about spatial relationships among
the parts of the figures will help students visualize
how to build these figures. Ask your child to tell
which of the polyhedra he or she is building in class
and to describe the process.

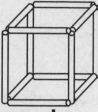

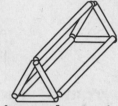

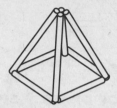

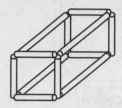

**cube**      **triangular prism**    **square pyramid**    **rectangular prism**

**1** Compare the cube and the rectangular prism.
Tell how they are alike and how they are different.

_____

_____

_____

**2** Compare the triangular prism and the square pyramid.
Tell how they are alike and how they are different.

_____

_____

_____

# Mixed Review and Test Prep

**3** $25¢ + 10¢ + 5¢ + 1¢ + 1¢ = \boxed{\phantom{00}}$

**A.** 52¢          **B.** 42¢          **C.** 37¢          **D.** 32¢

**Exploring Solids and Boxes**

# Follow Those Directions!

Sue and Tim followed these directions:

> Build a polyhedron that has
> 5 faces. Some of the faces
> should be triangles.

**Sue's polyhedron**

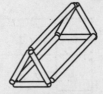

**Tim's polyhedron**

**1** Did Sue and Tim follow the directions?
If not, whose figure is wrong?

_____

**2** What could be added to the directions
so that only Sue's figure would be correct?

_____

**3** What could be added to the directions
so that only Tim's figure would be correct?

_____

# Mixed Review and Test Prep

**4** Helen took 47 paper clips from a box of 100 clips.
How many paper clips are left in the box?

**A.** 33      **B.** 43      **C.** 53      **D.** 63

**Exploring Solids and Boxes**

# Will It Make a Box?

Pam drew four patterns (see below).

**Family Connection**

Students have been using patterns to make boxes without tops that will each hold one cube. Working with these patterns helps students to visualize which patterns will form a box when cut out and folded, and which will not.

**1** Write the letters of the patterns that will make an open box when cut out and folded.

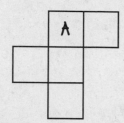

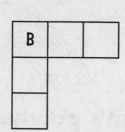

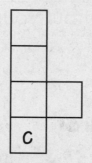

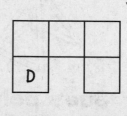

Patterns: _____

**2** Check your answers. Trace each pattern on another sheet of paper. Cut out each pattern and fold it. Did you choose the correct patterns?

_____

**3** Draw another pattern for an open box on the grid at the right.

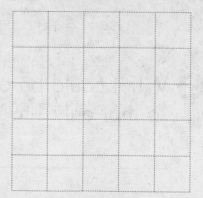

# Mixed Review and Test Prep

**4** Which can you use to solve this story problem?

> Sarah has 21 red marbles and 18 blue marbles. How many marbles does she have in all?

**A.** 21 − 8     **B.** 21 − 18     **C.** 21 + 8     **D.** 21 + 18

**Exploring Solids and Boxes**

# Looking at Pyramids

**①** Trace the pattern below on a blank sheet of paper.

**②** With crayons or markers, decorate each triangle any way you like. Then cut out your tracing and fold it to make a pyramid. Tape the edges so the shape stays closed.

**Family Connection**

As students investigate patterns for making solids, they learn about the faces of various solids and that there is more than one pattern for making any given solid. **Questions you might ask your child:** "Can you draw another pattern that would make the same pyramid as the one you just made?" "How are the faces of the two pyramids in Exercise 2 different?"

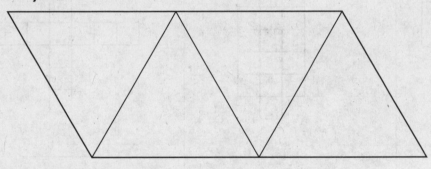

**③** Describe the faces of your pyramid. Then circle the pyramid at the right that best matches yours.

_____

_____

_____

# Mixed Review and Test Prep

**④** Find the missing number.   $12 + \boxed{\phantom{0}} = 23$

**A.** 11      **B.** 10      **C.** 9      **D.** 8

**Exploring Solids and Boxes**

# Box Patterns

Each of the six patterns below could be cut out and taped together to make a box without a top.

How many cubes would fit in each box?

**Family Connection**

Students are using 2-dimensional drawings of box patterns to determine how many cubes each pattern will hold after it has been cut out and folded into a 3-dimensional box. Ask your child to explain how he or she decided on the number of cubes each of these boxes would hold.

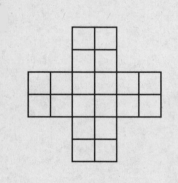

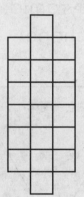

_____        _____        _____

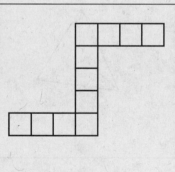

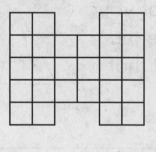

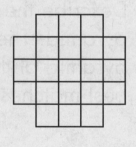

_____        _____        _____

# Mixed Review and Test Prep

Which number, when combined with 49, makes 100?

**A.** 48          **B.** 50          **C.** 51          **D.** 61

**Exploring Solids and Boxes**

# Be a Box Maker

**1** Draw two patterns for open rectangular boxes. One box should hold exactly 8 cubes and the other exactly 9 cubes.

**Family Connection**

Students are using square grids to design open rectangular boxes that will hold a given number of cubes. Ask your child to describe the strategy he or she used to design each box pattern on this page.

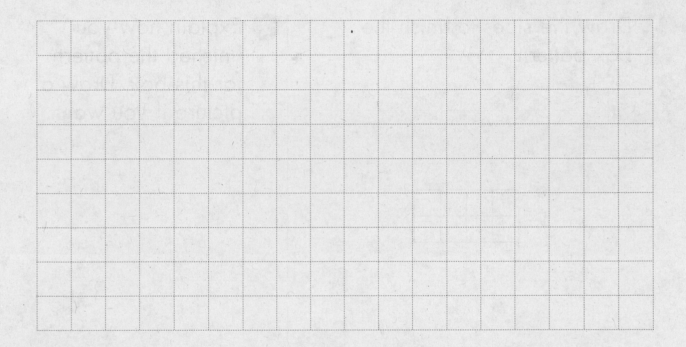

# Mixed Review and Test Prep

**2** Some students wrote the number of marbles they had on cards. They used the cards to make this graph. How many children have 5 marbles?

| | | | 5 marbles |
|---|---|---|---|
| 2 marbles | | 4 marbles | 5 marbles |
| 2 marbles | 3 marbles | 4 marbles | 5 marbles |

**A.** 8       **C.** 2

**B.** 3       **D.** 1

**Exploring Solids and Boxes**

# Building from the Bottom Up

The dark squares make the bottom of a rectangular box that contains exactly 24 cubes. The box has no top.

**Family Connection**
Students are completing patterns for boxes that will hold a given number of cubes. **Questions you might ask your child:** "Could you adjust the solution to complete a box pattern that would hold 16 squares?" "How would you do it?"

**1** Draw the sides to finish the box pattern.

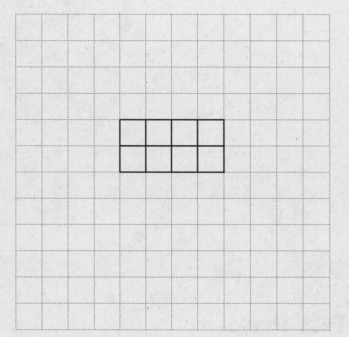

**2** Explain how you finished the pattern for this box. Draw a picture if you want.

# Mixed Review and Test Prep

**3** Mike needs $1 to buy a toy. He had 28¢. Then he earned 55¢ for helping in the house. How much **more money** does he need?

**A.** 17¢      **B.** 45¢      **C.** 72¢      **D.** 83¢

**Exploring Solids and Boxes**

# All Kinds of Boxes

These patterns make open boxes:

**Family Connection**

Students are building a city of open-box buildings as a class project. The buildings are made using box patterns like the ones shown here. Ask your child if he or she can tell you how to adjust any one of these patterns so that the box could hold another layer of cubes.

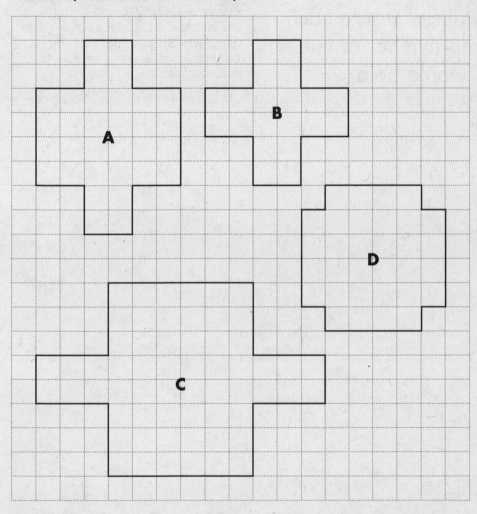

**1** Which box holds the greatest number of cubes? _____

**2** Which box is tallest? _____ Which is shortest? _____

## Mixed Review and Test Prep

**3** If each pencil costs 25¢, what is the cost of 3 pencils?

**A.** 75¢          **B.** 50¢          **C.** 35¢          **D.** 25¢

**Exploring Solids and Boxes**

# Three-Story Buildings

**1** Draw patterns for three different three-story buildings. Inside each pattern write the number of cubes each building would hold.

**Family Connection**

Students continue their work creating models of buildings using box patterns. **Questions you might ask your child:** "How did you find the number of cubes each of your 3-story buildings could hold? Do you have an easy way to find that number?"

# Mixed Review and Test Prep

**2** There are 28 students in Jerry's class. Nineteen students ride the bus to school. How many do not?

**A.** 4        **B.** 9        **C.** 12        **D.** 22

Name _____    Date _____

# City Planning

Write a letter to match each
of the architect's drawings
to a building in the city plan.

**Family Connection**

Part of the city planning project requires
your child to consider various types of
building designs. When driving through
your city or town, point out different
building styles and layouts. Ask your child
to think about why the buildings may
have been designed the way they were.

## Architect's Drawings

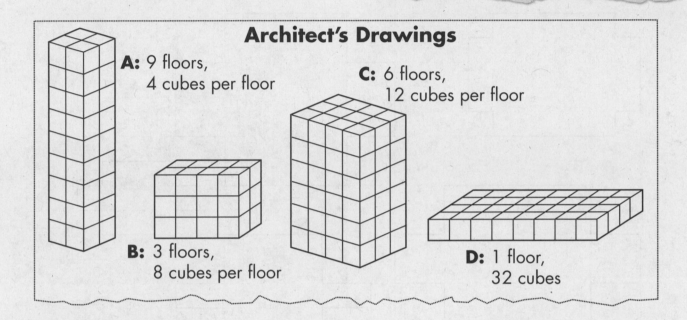

**A:** 9 floors,
4 cubes per floor

**C:** 6 floors,
12 cubes per floor

**B:** 3 floors,
8 cubes per floor

**D:** 1 floor,
32 cubes

## City Plan

**1** Office building, 36 cubes _____

**2** Shopping mall, 32 cubes _____

**3** Health clinic, 24 cubes _____

**4** Hotel, 72 cubes _____

**Interesting Tidbit**

The building in the
United States that has
the greatest amount
of total space inside
is located in Everett,
Washington. The
building is used to
assemble jumbo jets.

# Mixed Review and Test Prep

**5** Which number is 18 less than 90?

**A.** 108          **B.** 96          **C.** 78          **D.** 72

# Math City

Study these building
plans for Math City:

**Family Connection**

Students have completed a class project on building
cities. This activity shows a sample building plan.
Ask your child to describe each of the buildings by
telling you how many floors are in it and how many
cubes would fit on each floor.

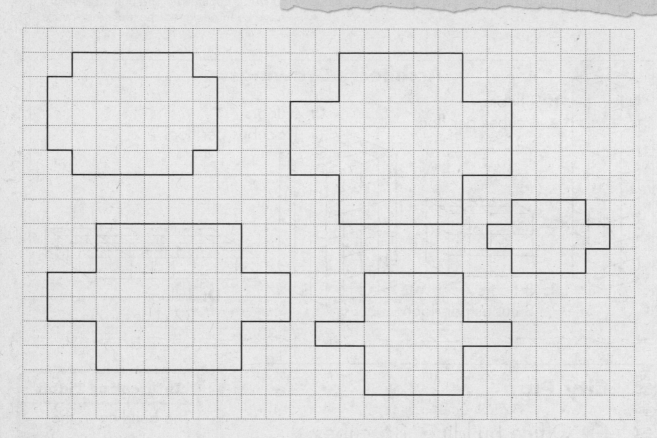

**1** How many cubes fit in the entire city? _____

**2** Explain how you found the answer.

_____

_____

## Mixed Review and Test Prep

**3** $17 - 14 = \boxed{\phantom{0}}$

**A.** 3          **B.** 5          **C.** 7          **D.** 13